FINDING MY VOICE

FINDING MY VOICE

Playing the fool, and other triumphs

JONATHAN VEIRA

MONARCH
BOOKS

Oxford, UK, & Grand Rapids, Michigan, USA

First published in the UK in 2012 by Monarch Books (a publishing imprint of Lion Hudson plc) and by Elevation (a publishing imprint of the Memralife Group):
Lion Hudson plc, Wilkinson House, Jordan Hill Road, Oxford OX2 8DR
Tel: +44 (0)1865 302750; Fax +44 (0)1865 302757; email monarch@lionhudson.com; www.lionhudson.com
Memralife Group, 14 Horsted Square, Uckfield, East Sussex TN22 1QG
Tel: +44 (0)1825 746530; Fax +44 (0)1825 748899;
www.elevationmusic.com

ISBN 978 0 85721 169 9 (print)
ISBN 978 0 85721 275 7 (Kindle)
ISBN 978 0 85721 276 4 (epub)
ISBN 978 0 85721 277 1 (PDF)

Distributed by:
UK: Marston Book Services, PO Box 269, Abingdon, Oxon, OX14 4YN
USA: Kregel Publications, PO Box 2607, Grand Rapids, Michigan 49501

The text paper used in this book has been made from wood independently certified as having come from sustainable forests.

British Library Cataloguing Data
A catalogue record for this book is available from the British Library.

Printed and bound in the UK by MPG Books.

For Sue and my boys –
Matt, Dan and Nick.
Forever loved.

Contents

Preface

Our human existence is nourished and entertained by the telling of stories, from *Treasure Island* to *Henry V*, from *Winnie the Pooh* to *The Lord of the Rings*.

Real life is packed with stories. All of us possess them, few of us have the privilege of recounting them again and again to people who are interested.

This book doesn't try to do anything but tell stories. My stories. Ultimately they are stories that involved many people in my frequent mishaps, momentous events and, often, just plain silliness.

To these people – my cast, if you will – I offer grateful thanks for being part of my life stories.

I have tried to remember every detail of the stories, but if I have remembered ever so slightly wrongly, then please forgive me. But know that, to the best of my ability, I have recorded what I remember.

I often read acknowledgments in books, and authors thank everyone including their great-great-grandmother.

I won't thank her but I would like to thank everyone who was involved either directly or indirectly in this project.

Ruth, my long-suffering sister, who sat for many days typing so many of these stories while I rattled them off at great speed. What an incredible skill – I am in awe. My brother-in-law Martin's frequent keen observations added so much.

Tim Pettingale, who sat with me for days, got me talking and helped me on the way.

Tony Collins, for believing that I had a story to tell in the first place.

Sue, who tirelessly, over many months, typed, corrected, corrected and typed. She also reminded me of forgotten details and told me to stop exaggerating. What a woman, what a wife!

Kate Matthews, for the frequent chats and stimulating thoughts.

Richard Everett, for his candid conversations and wisdom.

Andrew Wheeler, for encouraging me to write only what I believed in.

Adrian Plass, who encouraged me to "hold my nerve".

John Bathgate, for his sense of humour and the title.

Peter Martin and all the guys at Spring Harvest, for all their support.

Much of this was written three minutes' walk from where Dickens wrote *Bleak House*. If it was good enough for Dickens… Thanks to Jonathan and Alison for their wonderful, peaceful flat in Broadstairs.

To everyone mentioned and to those not mentioned, thanks for helping me to find my voice.

CHAPTER 1

Who Do You Think You Are?

What we remember from childhood we remember forever – permanent ghosts, stamped, inked, imprinted, eternally seen.

CYNTHIA OZICK

I magine the scene. I have just completed Verdi's major opera, *Falstaff*, at the Opera House in Oslo. I am exhausted from having sung for nearly three hours, and have received a rare standing ovation. I'm now back in the dressing-room. The dressers have taken off my "fat suit", which is dripping with sweat. I am sitting only in my underpants, make-up running down my face mingling with the sweat. I want a cool shower and a long drink.

Then through the door, without any warning, come my agent and her husband, their two friends, and the Italian Ambassador and his wife, whereupon I begin a normal conversation in Italian and English with the assembled throng. In my *underpants*...

Imagine, then, looking out for the first time (at the age of twenty-six) from the stage at Covent Garden, singing at *the* Glyndebourne Festival Opera in *Don Giovanni*; singing in the same opera in New Zealand with Dame Kiri Te Kanawa; performing at the Royal Albert Hall in the fortieth anniversary programme of *Songs of Praise* with Cliff Richard and Gloria Gaynor (both of whom are still alive!); singing for Princess Diana in *The Magic Flute* and having a charming conversation with her afterwards; sitting on the lap of the Duke of Kent during the same performance; standing inside 10 Downing Street as a guest of the Prime Minister; lunches with various members of the aristocracy... It has been a long, quirky journey for a plump, accident-prone boy from North-West London.

So, who do I think I am?

"Where are you from?"

"I'm from Harlesden."

"Yes, yes, but where are you actually *from*?"

This is the question most frequently put to me when people meet me for the first time. I suppose it's partly my brown skin and partly my name that makes people deeply curious. Origins are important. What I say loudly and proudly is, "I was born and bred in Harlesden, North-West London, England!" My *parents*, on the other hand, were born on a little island in the Caribbean Sea called St Vincent (where *Pirates of the Caribbean* was filmed). My mother was one of eleven children and my father was one of eight.

Both my parents were of mixed-race parentage. The name "Veira" is Portuguese and my father was Portuguese/Scottish/Irish. His mother (a Murphy) died tragically in an accident when he was a baby. My mother had a mixture of Irish, Scottish and Black African ancestry, and there seems to be very good evidence (after an exhaustive search by my Aunt Yvonne in Canada) of Native American blood as well! On top of all of this, some five years ago my optician told me I have astigmatism, which is common only to Chinese people! It may also help to explain why I love Chinese, Indian and West Indian food, together with the occasional haggis!

My father arrived in London first in 1955, followed by my mother in early 1957, when they got married. This was just a few years after the end of the Second World War, and in their new country rationing had only just finished and my father had to register for National Service (although he was never called up). He did serve in the Civil Defence Corps, however – something I only recently discovered. Britain, at that time, required a huge amount of rebuilding and called on the resources of the Commonwealth to assist her in this task. My parents were part of this and also, it has to be said, had little prospect for economic improvement in the West Indies. Other members of my mother's family had already arrived in the UK and therefore it was logical for my father to join them. Harlesden, at that time a little suburb of London, was their chosen destination. My memories as a child growing up there were of tree-lined avenues, safe streets, plenty of parks to play in and a great sweet shop around the corner!

Dad settled into a job at a factory owned by Smiths Industries, a local company which became the dominant supplier of instruments to British motorcar and motorcycle firms. Dad's official job title on my birth certificate states that he was a "grinder". This was one of the plethora of skilled jobs that were open to men who were prepared to work hard, including lots of overtime, for not very much money. That didn't change a great deal, even when he was promoted to setter. Later on, and I imagine much to his relief, he went to work for a very kind man named Frank Chattin as his manager in the estate agents, Chattin and Son. This was perched on the hill right next to Willesden Green tube station (and a great fish-and-chip shop). Here he had the opportunity to become established as an estate agent and, much later on, took over the business with my mother, with whom he made the endeavour a great success.

In those days we had no money to spare, even though Dad was at his workbench all the hours God sent. Mum had obtained a transfer from the bank where she worked in St Vincent to a bank in London. She stopped when my older sister Ruth was born, but eventually took a job as a secretary at Keble Memorial School, which my younger sister Jacqui and I later attended. Jacqui lives today just two minutes from where we were born.

In spite of those hard times, my memory is of a home that was constantly full of people. Sometimes we had visitors staying with us in our small two-bedroomed maisonette. Our home was always open to everyone – hospitality was simply a byword in our house and my parents showed it without reservation. What characterized our home was generosity and kindness. My father would – at the drop of a hat – help anybody to do anything. My mother just seemed to constantly cook and provide for family and friends. Looking back, I recognize that she often had little on her own plate. As far as my parents were concerned, lack of money was never a reason to say "No" to anyone. We would all "budge up" and another potato would go into the pot. In our own home now my wife and I try to do the same.

As a child I remember that we regularly had extra people with us for meals – particularly on Sundays. At Christmas time anyone who had nowhere else to go would come to us and be included in the family celebrations. Extra tables were squeezed into every corner of the dining room, the table groaning with various meats and vegetables... I can practically smell it now. Good days! We had a steady stream of "aunts" and "uncles" passing through the house – they weren't our relations but they filled that place in our lives.

Looking back, a couple who stood out for me were known to us as Auntie Edie and Uncle Ted. We were not related: we only got to know them because they moved into the maisonette above ours. But Uncle Ted, especially, became a key part of my life. So much so that I told stories to my children about him that they know as the "Uncle Tom stories". These would inevitably end up with Uncle Tom saving the day and everyone having a "slap-up meal". Uncle Ted was such a kind man – never, ever forgotten.

Children remember adults who pay attention to them. Ted and Edie were both our resident babysitters and our surrogate grandparents, teaching us to read, write and garden at a time when nurseries didn't exist. They didn't have any children of their own, so they were as happy to be with us as we were to be with them.

Uncle Ted was born in 1880. He would tell mesmerizing stories of a simpler time – such as how, as a young boy, he fell in the Thames and nearly drowned. "My whole life flashed before me, Johnny," he would say to me over and over again. He would tell me how, when that famous river froze, there would be a fair, right there on the ice. He would sit on our back doorstep while Mum brought him Camp coffee (coffee, but not as we know it), and he would pour it into the saucer to drink. In between sips he would dunk his rich tea biscuit, fishing it out with a spoon when it fell in.

He often picked me up from Furness Road School at the end of our road. He would regularly buy me an abundance of sweets from the corner shop: Lucky Bags, Refreshers, Black Jacks and Fruit Salads, not forgetting the fantastic Sherbet Dips. And who could forget the Strawberry Sherbets? They had a way of cutting the roof of my mouth to shreds, but boy, was it worth it! All of these I still prefer to this day to any of your posh, overpriced confectionery. Give me jelly babies over a Belgian chocolate any day. To Ted I owe my sweet tooth, and my diabetes!

Ted used to sing me old folk songs, thumping out the tune on his battered upright piano. I can still remember his voice, old but true, recalling a time when pianos in the home were commonplace and often the only entertainment. *Everyone* sang. Even though he died in 1973, when he was ninety-three and I was just thirteen, these memories are a significant part of me.

When he died, he was forty years into his second marriage. I remember the day he died. I was left holding the key to his front door, not allowed to go in because he was gone – just like that. I used to pop in after school most days; now he was not there. I went to his funeral and knew for the first time what the pain of bereavement feels like – as if your leg has been cut off. I had learned so many incidental life skills from Uncle Ted, such as the best way of cutting a piece of wood; picking up string from the postman's discarded bundle; looking for pennies dropped on the ground. (This skill came in very handy. One day I found a £5 note – a small fortune in the 1960s. My parents insisted that I took it to the police station, but as no one claimed it, it was mine to keep.) Now I also learned what death means: a presence, then an absence; a gain, then a loss. A picture of Uncle Ted and Auntie Edie remains on my bedroom window-sill to this day.

These are such vivid memories: Uncle Ted's stories,

his songs – I never got tired of hearing them. Occasionally he would sing me a music hall song that I've never forgotten: "Oh Lucky Jim (How I Envy Him)".

The first notes of a song and a love of storytelling. At its simplest, that is where opera begins, I suppose.

For many people, their first real encounter with the world of music was the descant recorder. Either you would avoid it in horror, thinking, quite rightly, that when any of your friends attempted to play it, the same recorder that had been sitting quietly minding its own business on a dusty shelf in the school music room, now sounded like a cat being slowly strangled. If you were among the unfortunate few, you were one of those children who practised with your long-suffering recorder teacher during a rainy playtime on a Thursday.

To me, the recorder is definitely an instrument of torture. Almost every child brings it home to play "London's Burning" until soon after, their parents wish with all their hearts that London *would* burn, and all recorders with it. In a survey, 92 per cent of parents asked said that they would happily pulp all recorders. (OK, I made that bit up.) My son Matt started on the recorder, but after 8 minutes 32 seconds we moved him directly on to the guitar.

However, if you get past the first faltering notes, you can learn to play rounds. If you stick at it, the humble recorder can teach you about counting and breathing properly. That's what the recorder did for me.

The islands of the Caribbean are full of music; you

are never far from a song, an elderly guitar or a ukulele. So when my parents came to England, they packed up their music and brought it with them. Dad played his battered old guitar and when I was four, I received a ukulele to add to my recorder. Then I mastered three chords – G, D7 and C. You can go a long way with three chords; all the way to rock and roll and home again.

On Sundays, however, we would pay a visit to a different kind of music: the music of the Plymouth Brethren.

Long before shops and pubs were open on a Sunday, families like mine would spend Sunday in church – all Sunday. We went to morning service, Sunday school in the afternoon, then the evening service. All that music, major and minor songs, and yet no instruments. No organ, no piano and certainly no guitar or, God forbid, drums. This particular branch of Christianity believed at that time that if the apostle Paul did not have instruments, then neither would they! All you needed was the words of a hymn and a good singer to lead. My dad would be the cantor, leading the song, pitching it by ear – occasionally too high or too low, but after initial fumbles we would all find the key. As the shepherd leads his flock over the hills and into the valley, we would settle on the natural harmony.

Music found my sisters and I everywhere. All three of us showed musical promise. Ruth was a natural on the piano. But probably because we had little money at that time, she never received lessons. I regret that for her, as I still remember hearing her playing *by ear* the pieces that Jacqui and I played from the music – an impressive skill that, sadly, she never had the chance to develop. However, Ruth acquired so many other skills that we don't have. Her keyboard and communication skills have been invaluable during the writing of this book.

Jacqui was a much better musician than me, much more naturally gifted. She was playing piano and flute concertos through her teen years; Mozart and all the masters. It's kind of ironic that I've ended up being the professional musician.

It sounds like we were a family straight out of *The Sound of Music*; in fact, people used to know us as "the Veira von Trapps". You could find us performing just about anywhere in and around North-West London – churches, women's meetings and old people's homes.

When I say "churches" I mean those strictly within our cluster of church families within the Plymouth Brethren. The Brethren was a strict church where every word of the Bible was studied in great detail. I learned so much of the Bible by heart. It was the first book I read. I still know by heart huge chunks from the Gospel of John. There is great poetry in the language. I learned how the sixty-six books follow each other, from Genesis to Revelation, to make up the Bible. Now that some time has elapsed between now and then, I can appreciate this part of my spiritual heritage. It is something that my kids just don't have.

My early faith included a lot of "Dos" and "Don'ts".

One of the "don'ts" was "Don't go to the picture house" – the cinema, in other words. As a kid, the only movie I remember seeing was *The Ten Commandments*, and even that was an undercover operation. This one-off foray into the land of Hollywood was made slightly less enjoyable by my parents' fear that someone from church would discover that we had been to the cinema. We snuck into the Hammersmith Odeon. I recall that part as I vividly remember breaking out a pair of purple flares for the occasion. Charlton Heston doing his Tablets of Stone stuff was mighty impressive and I loved seeing everything in Technicolor. That trip that gave me a real love of cinema which remains to this day.

In those days we were pretty much told that we were the chosen few. It seemed that the rest of Christendom had got it dreadfully wrong and that we chosen few were the only ones on the right track. There was a joke going round at the time that I rather liked:

> *Peter is giving a novice angel a guided tour of heaven. They come across a group of people making a huge amount of noise, banging tambourines.*
>
> *"Who are they?" asks the angel in surprise.*
>
> *"They are from the Salvation Army," replies Peter with a grin. Realizing he had better explain a bit more, Peter points out other groups to the puzzled angel.*
>
> *"Those guys with their hands up in the air*

*– they are the Charismatics. That lot kneeling
quietly over there with a book? They are the
Anglicans. Oh, and watch out for the Baptists –
they tend to be up to their waists in water, so they
get a bit wet."*

*Peter and the angel walk on until they come to
an imposing wall.*

*"Is anyone behind that wall?" the angel
enquires.*

*"Shhh! Don't say a word," Peter implores in
a hushed voice. "That's the Brethren. They think
they're the only ones here!"*

You can substitute almost any group for the Brethren.
We are all capable of thinking that we are the only ones
who are right. God forgive us!

The three of us once accompanied my parents to
a shelter for homeless people, to sing and preach to the
guys there – the bruised, the battered, the alcoholics, the
anonymous. We were singing away at the front of a lounge
of sorts, some people listening, some milling around. To
the right of us there was a man without shoes. While
my father was speaking, a guy from the other side of the
room – similarly dressed but with shoes – walked over.
With few words he removed his shoes and gave them to
the barefooted man. Without any fuss he returned to his
seat. It was an act of total selflessness, and everything I
thought the Christian faith should be about.

The Veira von Trapps would usually consist of

me on the piano, Jacqui on the flute or piano and Dad playing the guitar. With Mum and Ruth singing, it was a bit like Gladys Knight and the Pips! We seemed to sing naturally in three-, four- or even five-part harmonies. Nobody planned anything, we just did it. Only Jacqui and I read music, so there was no chance of anybody singing written-out stuff anyway. Practices were loud and fraught, with everyone thinking they knew how to make it sound better. It was my first experience of how not to practise – rehearsals cannot be a democracy! Very often my cousin, Simeon, who lived just around the corner, and had lived with us when he first came over to England, would also join us, adding an extra male voice and harmony and sometimes a guitar. Quite simply, music and singing were just part of all of our lives.

My first piano teacher's name was Rose Ely, a name that spoke of a generation far removed from my own. She wasn't all that old – no more than I am now, I fear – but I remember her as really ancient, old-fashioned and strict.

Rose was not child-friendly. To be fair, trying to get kids to learn something your way when they want to learn their way always has the potential to be torturous for both teacher and pupil. I liked playing by ear, and didn't read music easily. I've since figured out that I have a mild form of dyslexia and although I've improved, back then I couldn't easily link music to eye to fingers.

The disconnect did not end there. There was something of a gaping chasm between the repertoire that

Rose was dragging me through and the music that had captured my imagination via the magic of radio. Piano teachers continued to teach Mozart while my mates and I wanted to get into jazz or blues, Elton John or the Rolling Stones.

Rose's style of teaching revolved around shouting out commands to me from the back of the room:

"C major right hand, F major left hand… No, it's one flat, that's correct… No, that's *wrong*." This was all to the weird accompaniment of her crunching on raw carrots and lettuce, which I found strange as she was the size of a small European country. I concluded that she must have eaten the chocolate after we left.

At the time I remember thinking what a useless teacher she was, even though she worked for Trinity College of Music, so patently she wasn't useless. I remember going for my first exam, only to discover that she had neglected to tell me what to take, so I turned up with nothing only to be sent home again. It was an utterly terrifying experience for a nine-year-old boy.

Rose was convinced that I did not practise at home and berated me about it constantly. The reality was that my parents had somehow scraped together enough funds to go out and buy a piano for us. But none of us knew enough to realize that the top notes were missing – it was a *miniature* piano. My mother favoured this particular piano because she loved the case-work and thought it looked good! Fair enough. I eventually, gratefully, inherited it and I believe it is now being used in a school in Croydon, which is fantastic. You don't really own pianos, you just take care of them until the next user comes along.

Actually, the missing keys weren't so bad at first. They only became a problem when I started playing more technical pieces, say Khachaturian's *Toccata*, which has a lot of notes in the upper register of the keyboard. I would compensate by playing the lower octave twice – you have to manage with what you have.

In contrast, my sons have a choice of pianos to play. But back then my parents had really struggled to afford both a piano and lessons. They saved hard and bought things when they had the money. They gave me something beyond price, and to this day I am very grateful to them both.

Some are born with the gift. There are those who apply themselves and master something that other people do not have the inclination or motivation for, like horse riding, golf or the piano. And then there are prodigies – people who are highly gifted, with a talent so rare as to inspire wonder.

One of the wonders of prodigy is that it finds children as young as four, able to sit down at a piano and play exactly what they hear. Some of these kids will go on, seemingly without effort, to read the most exquisitely complicated sheet music and play as if heaven were to be found among the black and white keys. Some will compose the kind of pieces that others, who are much older and who have practised much harder, will play with humble appreciation.

I am not a prodigy. From day one I have felt ever so slightly inadequate to the task of mastering all those light and dark notes, careful to negotiate all the twists and turns, just about hanging in there, smiling while others glide past me in the fast lane, feeling like a learner driver at a Grand Prix.

More than anything I like to improvise, to find a chord and then look for a second one that adds texture to the first, taking a song somewhere you might not expect it to go. Even as a kid, that's what I wanted to do.

I did, however, seem to understand music in some sort of preordained, precocious, wholly organic way. For whatever reason, my ability to detect errors in a song or a classical performance was as finely tuned as the hearing of a bat. This skill would drive my parents to distraction. Regularly we would be listening to someone playing on the radio, only for precocious little me to gleefully point out all the bits that were wrong. They would give me the look that only parents can pull off – the quizzical "How would *you* know it's wrong?" kind of look – while feeling the instinctive need to put me right on the subject:

"There's absolutely nothing wrong with this!" they would say.

I would bash on like a little annoyed Beethoven:

"Everything is wrong with it. It's not correct, it's not good, it hasn't got musicality and, to add insult to injury, it is notationally JUST PLAIN BAD!"

It must have been the equivalent of having a chef like Marco Pierre White, as a young boy, sitting at your lunch table. You can imagine the comments as a lovingly prepared tuna mayonnaise sandwich is placed before him:

"The bread is at least a day old, the mayo is not home made and the tuna… is that from a tin?"

Apologies to Marco, who was probably the height of discretion as a pre-teen. I, on the other hand, was not. I had great error detection and not so great piano playing skills, a frustrating combination. Hence, when I could not play what I was hearing in my head, I would always default to singing it. I still do it now. If, during a concert, I play something and it's not quite right, I sing along. I suppose this is my way of saying, "This is how it should be, so please forgive my inability to play it like it should be played."

Pianists are always checking out other pianists. I guess this is the same for anyone trying to improve how they do something. Professional musicians are always looking for the smoke and mirrors or the sleight of hand in a performance. In the same way, movie directors do not simply settle down with their oversized popcorn and overpriced drink at someone else's movie and simply enjoy the story. They are looking at the camera angles, the lighting, the continuity errors.

As a kid it was pure magic listening to the likes of Dave Brubeck or Elton John. Elton was the epitome of cool: a classically trained pianist who had somehow managed to take all those hours of practice and turn them into a rock song. The piano fairly sang for him. Then there was Billy Joel, again classically trained, writing intelligent songs about working-class stuff and bashing his piano about like a boxer. To this day I puzzle over why Billy Joel didn't, and doesn't have more street "cred". All the credibility seemed to be thrown lovingly at the feet of Bob Dylan, and I'm going to whisper this for fear of having old fruit lobbed at me: I don't get Bob Dylan – except occasionally. OK, I've said it.

I recorded one of Dylan's gospel songs – "Gotta Serve Somebody" – from an album of his that I do get, *Slow Train Coming*. Blues-based gospel, I love it. But "Blowin' in the Wind"? Personally, I would let it alone in the wind to dry out.

As a boy growing up in London in the 1960s and 1970s I was a dreamer. I loved the escape world of comics: Superman, Batman, the Incredible Hulk and the Flash. I would have arguments with other boys about who was the strongest, fastest and best. I loved Westerns and gunfights where the goodie in the white hat always won. I used to spend a lot of time drawing guns and holsters. I imagined myself to be "The One" who was the hero and would save the damsel in distress.

I played a lot of make-believe games, which included a game that ended in disaster and extra work for my father! In this game I imagined a burglar breaking into the house. I would draw my two cap-guns and hold him prisoner until the police arrived. I would (of course) be acclaimed as the hero of the day. What this involved in practical terms was me tying a piece of string from the door handle onto my old-fashioned light-switch. I spent a long time making this secure and practising my role in slow motion. The burglar would walk into my bedroom and, in so doing, would pull the door shut behind him, turning the light on and trapping himself in the room, secured by the string around his neck. At which point I would pull out my pistols and keep him there until the police came.

This was all very well until I went for my bath (it must have been a Friday: we only had baths on a Friday). As always, I ran at high speed out of the bathroom and into my bedroom, not thinking. The trap did its job. The door closed, the light went on and, unfortunately, at the same time the light-switch was ripped out of the wall, together with a massive part of the wall itself – plaster, wallpaper and everything from light-switch to skirting-board! I stood there stunned, just thinking, "Dad will kill me for sure!" Strangely, my father arrived on the scene without the police, and to this day I can't figure out why he was so calm and silent, and with that look on his face that said, "How on earth have you managed to make this mess?"

Years later, in his speech at my and Sue's wedding, my father-in-law affectionately described me as having an "accident-prone appetite". In other words, accidents just seemed to follow me around!

I have continued to confirm his opinion throughout

my life. On one occasion I was staying at lodgings in Buxton. I was performing in the Buxton Festival and renting a room in a lovely Edwardian town-house in the town centre. The landlord was a delightful man – very friendly and proud of his beautifully kept establishment.

One day I was luxuriating in the bath when a fellow lodger asked me through the door if he had left his wedding ring on the bathroom shelf. I stood up to look and yes, there it was. As I did, however, suddenly there was a loud *crack*, the bath split open end to end, and water began pouring out through the gap! In panic I leapt out of the bath and started trying to bail the water out of the bath with the only receptacle I could find: a small soap dish. Back and forth I ran across the cavernous bathroom, throwing the contents of the tiny soap dish into the sink. The fellow lodger was outside wondering what was going on and I was streaking back and forth shouting in dismay as the water disappeared down the crack. I didn't think of unplugging the bath Then, throwing a towel around me, I rushed downstairs to see where the bathwater had ended up.

It had poured through the ceiling and into the dining room below. My landlord had only been showing me his beautiful, newly lacquered table that very morning. Now it was drenched in the contents of my bath. I do not know what foresight had prompted him, but the landlord had covered the table just hours before... with a waterproof cloth. As I stood there dripping in the dining room, I spluttered my apologies.

"Oh, not to worry, Jonathan, it must have been my fault," my kind host reassured me. "I installed that bath and didn't put the required number of supports in place."

Indeed – an appetite for accidents. That seems to be a part of who I am.

CHAPTER 2

Mixed Blessings

Do you not see how necessary a world of pains and troubles is to school an intelligence and make it a soul?

JOHN KEATS

One of the most exciting, daunting and challenging parts of my life as an international opera singer has been the "international" bit. I have travelled to twenty-seven different countries, and it has been interesting, to say the least. Airports swiftly lose any glamour when travelling for business, especially since 9/11 and the advent of serious security measures, which are wholly necessary – apart from the water thing! Some bottled-water company somewhere is making a huge amount of money out of us. The security measure is simply "Drink the water at security and if you die, then obviously you can't take the flight"! Travelling has become a largely unpleasant experience. Most of the officials in airports clearly seem to have had a charisma and humour bypass.

Surely frisking somebody can be fun? Airports become as one, whether Berlin, Heathrow, Paris, Copenhagen, Oslo or Auckland.

This last airport however, opened a significant door for me and subsequently for my whole family. In 1993 I was invited to go and sing the role of Papageno in Mozart's opera *The Magic Flute*, as a direct result of singing the same role at the Covent Garden Festival earlier that year. My wife Sue had left me a message on a bit of paper by the telephone after receiving a call from Helen, my agent. It simply read: "Magic Flute, N2" – or so I thought. Like an idiot, I assumed that this was a place in North London (N2) and not, as it was, in Auckland, New Zealand (NZ).

It was very exciting, however, because I had never performed in the Antipodes before. I was thirty-three, very enthusiastic, and international travel still held a fascination for me. The sad thing for me was that my youngest son, Nick, was barely three months old when I left, and hardly knew me when I came home about three months later.

On the plus side, the company was paying for me to travel business class on Air New Zealand, which meant that I sat upstairs and had all the privileges that went with travelling in business. I had decided to travel all in one go, which meant fourteen hours to LA, a two-hour refuelling stopover and off again for another fourteen hours or so. I couldn't sleep for the whole time on the aeroplane and arrived having travelled almost continually for thirty-two hours. On arrival at Auckland International at 6 a.m. local time, I was met by an incredibly friendly representative from the opera company. She took me straight to the apartment that I would be staying in for the next nine and a half weeks. She was concerned that I would need a day to get over the jet lag. It had been a truly gruelling journey – something I wouldn't choose to do again in a hurry. But for some reason I was wide awake and raring to go, so she took me shopping. Then she asked me if I was ready for some sleep.

"No, no, no. When do the rehearsals begin?" I retorted perkily.

"10.30 a.m.," said she.

"Let's go and meet the people and see what we can do," I replied with what must have seemed like drug-induced enthusiasm!

In I went and met the lovely team of singers, the conductor and the director. The conductor asked if I wanted to sing.

"Let's do it," I said.

I then did a full rehearsal until 5.30 p.m., arriving back at my apartment an hour later. I had now been up for approximately forty-five hours since leaving London.

"This is strange," I thought. "I feel so wide awake!"

Then, all I can remember is going to stand by the bed, fully clothed.

"That's the bed," I thought.

Suddenly and involuntarily, I fell forward and woke up thirteen hours later in exactly the same position, fully clothed. I had never experienced my body "switching off" like that before.

The opera went exceptionally well for me: the company was very pleased with my performances and the reviews were very complimentary. It was a great production and I loved working with these guys. New Zealanders are such "can do" people. As one of them said, "When you are 12,000 miles away from Europe, you are free to try almost anything."

This success led to an invitation by the director of the opera company, Stephen Dee, for a return visit to sing in the opera *Don Giovanni*, in one of my favourite roles, Leporello. More excitingly, I would be singing with the world-famous Dame Kiri Te Kanawa in the role of Donna Elvira. It was a role she was famous for performing all over the world as well as recording. This, by strange coincidence, was the role that I saw her perform in a film of *Don Giovanni* that Sue and I saw on our first date in 1980. I remember turning to Sue at that time and saying how incredible it would be to sing the role of Leporello with this lady. We both laughed heartily, as this seemed so far from my grasp. But here I was in 1993, being offered the chance to perform with the Dame herself. Sometimes I love this job!

Stephen Dee and I began our negotiations at a restaurant in the centre of Auckland, where I suddenly hatched a scheme to not only get me over there, but also the whole family. I had arrived with a list in my pocket of what I required from him. It all relied on my ability to barter and not blink before I got close to the deal I wanted. Stephen was a brilliant negotiator, but eventually we both ended up with a highly satisfactory package. I phoned Sue almost immediately and she of course got hooked into the idea! We started making plans for what would be a great family adventure and an experience that would create some of our fondest and most enduring family memories. In fact, two of our three boys have individually returned to NZ during their gap years, and as I write Nick is planning a trip there. They returned to Orewa, where we lived in the house of Frank, a Friend of Auckland Opera and our long-suffering landlord! A wonderful woman, our neighbour Glenda, has become my boys' Kiwi mum – she has taken them and their travelling companions into her home and made her way straight into their hearts. The kindness of strangers!

So in January 1996 the whole family – Matt (eight), Dan (four) and Nick (two) – travelled 12,000 miles (via one week in Los Angeles for the obligatory Disneyland trip) before I began work with Kiri. It was a huge trip for a family of five with nine pieces of baggage. Sadly, with all the luggage we forgot the buggy, which wasn't helpful with Nick deeply asleep at the airport! I remember Matt, even at the age of eight, being brilliant, helping to carry baggage and doing anything that he could to assist. It is a trait that he displays to this day. Dan was his usual quiet, undemanding self.

It was an awesome experience working with such a

legend as Kiri. We quickly became friends and she was heard to say about my first meeting with her, "He's a cheeky one, isn't he?"

The rehearsal period was relatively short and I had a suspicion that Kiri did not particularly buy into the production. I know how this feels now, having done a role so many times. You have your own ideas about how it should go and, more importantly, how it shouldn't go. After much struggle and a few beautifully performed tantrums from many of us, the show began. The first night was a success. The sell-out audiences who had come to see Dame Kiri were more than satisfied with what they saw and heard.

I think it was during the second performance that something went drastically wrong. The opera was set in the 1930s for the purposes of this production. This meant, for example, instead of the Commendatore being killed in a seventeenth-century sword fight, he was killed by a massive truck rolling onto the set. The set was on two levels, so the action could take place simultaneously.

On this particular night I was on the lower level, hidden behind two large dustbins. The dustbins enabled us to get to the back of the set without being seen by the audience. They were so big that we could climb into them. We had rehearsed that I would pop up from one dustbin, like Animal in *The Muppet Show*, and Don Giovanni would pop up from the other. We needed to swap clothes for the famous trio with Donna Elvira. I was doing my quick change before my re-entry to the set, which meant that I had exactly one minute and twenty seconds to change from *my* costume into the Don's. The music had begun. I had one ear on the orchestra and one eye on the costume. Unfortunately the dresser made a mistake with one of the sleeves and I was momentarily distracted. As I inclined my ear once more to the orchestra I thought I heard my cue. I took what was left of the costume in my hands, thinking I would put it on later, since I couldn't be late for my musical entry:

"Zitto di Donna Elvira!" ("Quiet, it's Donna Elvira!")

Having popped up, I looked out to the assembled 3,500 people and started singing my line. Unfortunately for me, I was three bars of music too early. The conductor, Stephen Barlow, did what was customary on these occasions and put up his left hand in a motion very similar, if not identical, to a policeman stopping traffic. It said:

"Stop singing, stop singing now, you are in the wrong place at the wrong time. STOP IT!"

However, the lovely man, Michele Bianchini, who was playing the Don, thought to himself, "I will help him and be a good colleague."

Thus he popped up from his dustbin and began to sing where he thought his line began. This was also incorrect and Stephen dutifully put up his right hand aimed at the unfortunate Don. Two commands to stop singing for both of us. I glanced to my right and saw that Kiri (who *should* have been singing at that point) had been so messed up by us and was laughing so much that she had to turn away from the audience. All I could see were her shoulders going up and down in helpless laughter. Eventually, Stephen, out of a sense of desperation, hearing no singing whatsoever, made a motion with both of his hands in a downward position – a clear visible sign that he had given up on all three of us. He shook his head in frustration, indicating resignation to the whole sorry, sad affair. Being the professionals we were, however, halfway through the trio, we found our way back and completed that section without further incident. The audience, as is often the case, were completely unaware of our faux pas. When off stage, however, we laughed nervously, loud and long.

It has to be said that Stephen was not so amused and made that quite clear in the interval. Needless to say, it didn't happen again – and the dresser responsible was left in no doubt about how JV felt!

New Zealand is an extraordinary place and it possesses a charm all of its own. I have not experienced such openness and a sense of belonging anywhere else apart from England.

However, I didn't always fit in. As I write this, I have just received from someone on Facebook a picture from my school magazine of 1972/1973. I was on the front together with six or seven others. I had hair, my tie was knotted correctly, and I was smiling. On the other hand, that snapshot doesn't tell the full story of my schooldays.

Where did that phrase come from, "School – the best days of your life"? I'm guessing either from someone who has a hazy memory of the bits that were not all that rosy, or perhaps someone for whom it was all sunshine and friendly kick-abouts in the school playground. For the rest of us, that phrase can have the same dampening effect as equally shiny, happy-people phrases such as, "Look on the bright side" or "Every cloud has a silver lining". No, it doesn't – every cloud has the potential to soak you to the skin. *My* school days were decidedly *not* the best days of my life.

Imagine you are approached to write a book about your life. What bits would you want to gloss over or leave out altogether? Maybe because those bits are too painful, or too intimate, or because they could be misinterpreted. The difficult thing for me about writing this book has been what to include and what to leave out. Sometimes, as an actor and performer, it is difficult to know where the real me starts and ends.

Putting on make-up can help me to get into character, but the essential thing is to remember to take it off. At Glyndebourne, when I was in the opera *Lulu* by Alban Berg, I finished my performance and, in my hurry to get out and home, I completely forgot that I had glitter, false eyelashes and *very* rosy cheeks. I went to pay for petrol in the garage down the road and said in my best North London brogue, "Pump number seven, mate." The attendant was sniggering behind the counter and eventually I asked him what his problem was. He said,

"Have you seen your face, mate?" Then I remembered. I tried to explain but I don't think he believed me. Anyway, we all have a face that we don for public consumption.

I am mixed race. Even those words, "mixed race", can be difficult. If you are mixed, then by definition you are neither one thing nor another; you are a combination of individual cultures, separate experiences and other colours.

I think that when you start out being different, you often want nothing more than to fit in, because you don't feel like you belong anywhere specific. You can be left feeling disconnected, on the outside looking in. As an adult, with the benefit of having come to understand much more about how life and people work, you can begin to embrace the benefits of your differences. But as a kid, this is tough.

I am what I am, but that has not always been easy to live with. The facts: approximately 92 per cent of the UK is not brown. So fifty years ago, when the brown population was a lot lower, I didn't exactly fit in. I acutely remember going to Scotland with my parents on holiday when I must have been twelve or thirteen (1973 or so), and I went to play bowls with my dad (who is not brown). The lady handing out equipment said to my dad, in front of me, "Does your friend speak English?"

Yes, indeed I do, madam, and proper English at that. As human beings, it is natural for us to suspect anything that is different – a protection mechanism that we all have. Those of us who are "outsiders" expend an awful lot of energy trying to fit in and be one of the boys. I suppose it was partly why I developed the knack of changing accents to suit whatever situation I was in, whether as a boy in North London with a group of hard young thugs about to beat me up, or the Prime Minister, David Cameron at Downing Street, or the bloke in the Indian restaurant (nearly got into trouble with that one), or the customs officer in St Lucia, or on BBC Radio Belfast with John Bennett the presenter. Fitting in, you see, has always been important to me, rightly or wrongly. It is hard to convey what an impact this has, but anyone who has had difficulty fitting in for any reason will know what I am talking about.

Fitting in can be very costly. After an internal debate about how to tell this part of my story, I decided to tell it like it was. As a child, I got beaten up, several times. I remember being chased down the road in Kilburn, being called a "Paki". I got a brick hurled at my back and I still have the scar to prove it. I got mugged at knifepoint at Willesden Junction Station, mugged for money while being called every vicious name under the sun. Sticks and stones may break your bones, but words can make wounds that are equally difficult to heal. Give me a stick or a stone any day. Words leave their indelible mark.

I got good at talking my way out of trouble. On one occasion I recall being surrounded by a large group of teenagers and talking my way out of that situation – I basically started a discussion group there and then. That confused them. I think they are probably still there, discussing the virtues of racist attacks. Well, maybe not. Occasionally, in more recent years, I have again been the target for inexplicable venom. I love Belfast and I never usually have any problems there at all. On the contrary. But once, when I was on the phone to Sue, a group of skinheads found me and started *zieg heil*-ing in my face, while I was talking to her. The language is always much the same, mainly one-syllable words spat out of a thin mouth with a clenched jaw.

I had to hang up on my wife, who was left not knowing, only imagining. Mercifully, a police van came past at that moment, a miracle for which I am truly grateful. That was about eighteen years ago.

Yet school is such a big part of a child's experience. If you don't count sleeping, a child spends as much, if not more, time at school with their fellow pupils and teachers as they do with their family. Five days a week, every week, not counting holidays and sick days. Depressing, if you don't like school.

The school I remember most is St Augustine's in Kilburn. Before that I was at Furness School, Harlesden and then Keble Memorial, where my mum was that figure we all knew and loved: the school secretary. The only memories I have of Furness are these: it was just around the corner from our house and I won a couple of poetry competitions there. Best days of my life, there you go. If you only talk about the good bits you can say it with meaning! At any rate, I must have said my poem with meaning, because I won a Furness award for it. It was based on the John Betjeman poem, "Harrow On The Hill". My poem, more suited to my age group and encompassing a handy reference to a popular film of the time, went something like this:

> *The train goes running down the line,*
> *Chitty bang, chitty bang,*
> *I wish it were mine,*
> *Chitty bang, chitty bang,*
> *I wish it were mine.*

That was the first time I knew I could do something. I stood up, said my piece and something good happened as a result. That award meant a lot to me. It was similar to the sense of achievement you would feel upon successfully climbing a difficult rock-face, reaching a break in the clouds. The magic moment when suddenly you could see where you were and you liked being there.

St Augustine's in Kilburn was one of the smaller schools in the area. Mum and Dad were keen for me to go there instead of to one of the other schools in the area, which were very large and not church schools. I was not hugely academic, but bright enough to do OK. Even so, I was nervy in the classroom and positively terrified in the playground. They played a game called "champ" that was a mixture of handball and Rollerball! I was decidedly *not* good at this and soon found out to my detriment.

For many kids, the playground can be the equivalent of being sent outside three times a day to fight a battle of wits, strength and endurance. One of the many names that got thrown at me out there, along with a fist when no one was looking, was "Turkey". I was more on the rounded than the twig side, so "Turkey" was a playground joke at my expense, like they were fattening me up for Christmas or something. I would laugh along with it, hoping they would eventually forget me and move on to someone else.

Apart from the obvious differences that kids will use against each other to effortlessly manifest playground tension, such as a kid's colour, size, teeth, hair or even their laugh, I stood out in other ways. We were pretty sheltered at home: restricted TV, bed by seven, church on Sunday. I had little in common with the kids I was at school with. They were much more streetwise than me and I must have been an oddball, to say the least. I had no hope of fitting in.

I was always at least a step away from knowing about the latest TV show or wearing the right clothes. My parents had neither the money nor the inclination to buy the "in" gear that guarantees acceptance in school. If winklepickers were the thing, Mum would be able to afford the shoes that were cool before winklepickers, say brogues. If brogues were in vogue, Mum would be able to afford winklepickers. Things like what shoes you wore and how wide or narrow your trousers were mattered enormously. I had my one pair of purple flares and that was it!

Now I have three children of my own and it is no

different. Clothes are still an issue, but my kids don't care about that. "Do you have a mobile? What model is it? What Playstation/Xbox have you got?" As you get older, that can morph into the adult version: driving the right car, living in the right part of town. I just do not think your life or mine benefits from the kind of sizing up and labelling that we learned back in the playground. Labels drive people apart more than they bring them together. I have no idea what labels are in or not, fashionable or not. If you buy your clothes from Asda or Jaeger, I truly don't care, even now.

At this point, if I was going to leave school with anything at all, I would need a miracle. My miracle arrived in the form of a man called Ian Lawrence – a life saver. He was a short but powerful Scot, but not the "Och aye the noo" type. I think he was about four feet six or so! I remember so well the first time I encountered him. It was in the music room. My class were a rabble. We were standing outside making a terrible noise and generally doing what our class did best – not a lot! He came out and demanded silence before we went into the class in two orderly lines. He demanded silence as we sat and he wrote on the blackboard:

> *I will bring to Mr Lawrence's lessons:*
> *A pencil (sharp)*
> *A rubber (clean)*
> *A ruler (not broken).*

We copied this and other stuff down into our exercise books and the boy next to me, one Andrew Waker, said, "He's a right little Hitler, isn't he?" Well, that so-called "little Hitler" went on to become (to the bemusement of other staff) by far the most popular and respected teacher in the school, and my wee miracle. He was a phenomenal teacher and remains a family friend to this day.

All the energy I had, day in and day out, was spent on surviving, keeping my head above water, only to have it pushed under again. Ian saw what was going on and somehow, instinctively knew where I was at. Then he threw me a lifebelt. He gifted me with the key to his study and to the music room, along with these amazing words:

"Why don't you go in there and practise at playtimes?"

Ian had rescued me from the playground and played a significant role in making me aware of the possibilities beyond those walls that, left to my own devices, I would never have contemplated.

The careers advice at our school was about as life-enhancing as flatulence in a spacesuit. Most of the kids at our school would be advised to become white-collar workers or carpenters. Sadly, my talents didn't lie in any of these areas – particularly not in the area of carpentry. I am sure that Uncle Ted turned in his grave!

For my GCSE Woodwork (equivalent) I had to make an Anglepoise-type lamp in a day. I spent the first four and a half hours gluing together the bits that I had inadvertently broken and waiting for them to dry. The teacher came across to me and said famously, "Veira, boy, I do hope you are good at something else!" Predictably, I got an unclassified grade at GCSE Woodwork, which is just about as bad as not turning up for the exam at all.

If you were working class, the traditional way of avoiding jobs like clerical work or carpentry was to become a footballer, a boxer or, by the sixties and seventies, a rock star. If I'm honest, I was more interested in becoming a rock star than anything else, and even less convinced that university was a credible option for me. But Ian continued to encourage me to try for university, the golden ticket that no one in my family had ever been able to consider, let alone attain. While my family was worrying about when I was going to get a "proper job", Ian gave me the confidence to break the mould, to see a different way of looking at life and its possibilities.

St Augustine's was a state school and until recently had been a grammar school. It was one of the new, exciting, modern, all-purpose, comprehensive schools that made up the Inner London Education Authority (ILEA).

As part of an attempt to generate a New World Order for education starting in Inner London, the ILEA was funnelling comparatively large amounts of money into music at my school. We had a whole wing dedicated to music and it was stupendous, even by today's standards. A Steinway stood proudly in the shiny new lecture theatre, partner to all six feet seven of another grand piano in a nearby hall. Then there were four rehearsal rooms, each with a pretty good piano and some with two pianos, so you and your teacher could double up if you so chose.

I had other choices now. I could choose to go out into the playground and pretty much guarantee that I would get beaten up, or I could take my pick of pianos while the other kids got on with working out their pecking order. Guess which appealed the most?

Along with the spirit of ILEA's musical benevolence came offers of free instrument tuition for kids who would not have been able to afford private lessons. You could take your pick – piano, string or wind instruments – and a teacher would be found for you. Loads of kids got to take a significant musical step up because of this initiative. We were pushed to achieve at the highest standard and encouraged to perform constantly. All classical, mind you – no *X Factor* nonsense. (As an aside, it always makes me laugh when I see someone do something very average on *X Factor* and people go wild. Trust me, there is a dedicated bunch of talent out there that will never be seen on the *X Factor*.)

I tried all the instruments on offer: flute, clarinet, violin, viola. Not brass, though, because my parents thought it would be too loud. Possibly a wise decision, given that the school would let us take instruments home and bearing in mind the size of our living space. I became reasonably accomplished on the clarinet and viola. My sister Jacqui, who attended the same school, continued to progress hugely on the piano and very soon equally so on the flute. My piano teacher, David Wyatt, encouraged in me a "no tolerance of mediocrity" attitude which remains to this day. For this I am thankful.

My piano practice would always start out classical and tilt towards rock for the last joyous fifteen minutes. I would toy with and copy songs from Elton John that I had heard on the radio under my pillow the night before – "Your Song", for example, or the theme tunes to TV programmes such as *Van der Valk*, or film scores like "The Entertainer" from *The Sting* – that one went down well. I particularly liked the effect that certain songs had on girls, something no classical piece seemed to be able to produce. Girls liked sad songs, like Frankie Valli and the Four Seasons' "My Eyes Adored You", or David Gates and Bread's "Diary" – simply one of the most depressing and self-indulgent songs ever written. I loved it! I took to playing in the main school hall because it was right by the music department, had great acoustics, a proscenium arch and, best of all, girls, who would walk through to get to PE or music lessons.

I would be playing a piece by Mozart or Bach until a girl appeared, then I'd break into Frankie Valli. Soon I would have an audience, someone wanting an encore. Music draws people. It has a life all of its own. It can alter a mood easier than anything and it can change the way you think. Then, as soon as they disappeared, back to Mozart!

The first time I remember venturing up on stage to perform for an audience at school it was me, my dad's guitar and my version of "Mother of Mine" by little Jimmy Osmond – an A-minor tear-jerker that had my mum weeping copious tears throughout. I got to the end feeling very pleased with myself, but thinking, "Oh Mum, pleeeze!"

What followed was many musical concerts, playing the piano, singing in choirs and so on. Ian encouraged us to do more than we thought was possible. It always felt like over-reaching, but we loved it and it made us into the musicians we are today. Slightly later on in my school career, I entered the strange world of the School Musical (what is known now as a "Glee Club") by playing Dr Grimwig in a production of *Oliver Twist*. Some time after this, in 1977, when I was sixteen, I was offered the plum role of the King in *The King and I*. I could tell from the title of this production that the role of the King was going to be much more taxing than my "enter stage right, say your lines and leave" contribution as Dr Grimwig. I was worried about it and did my best to convince Ian Lawrence that I couldn't pull it off, the conversation running a little like the popular Irving Berlin song "Anything You Can Do I Can Do Better", except in reverse:

"No I can't."

"Yes you can."

"No I can't!"

"Yes you can!"

I had a small stutter and retain it to this day when in pressured situations, in TV interviews and the like. I didn't speak that much, so the thought of all those words was, mildly speaking, petrifying. Eventually I did it, still kicking and screaming behind the scenes. I learned the lines and I pulled it off.

The costumes for that play were lovingly crafted by the Needlework Department. I got huge, handmade, elasticated pantaloons and a tiny waistcoat. There is a big scene somewhere in the middle of the story when the King inspects all his children and the last little nipper is meant to draw attention to himself by gently tugging *on the side* of the old King's trousers. Of course, it being my school, the little twit had more devious plans and pulled *down* my pantaloons to reveal my psychedelic Marks & Spencer's Y-fronts. I'm sure Yul Brynner never had that problem.

Having survived the pantaloons drama, I summoned all my acting skills for the scene where the King finally expires. School props being what they were, I got to die on a humble camp bed draped with a blanket that was not long enough to cover my feet. My mum sat in the audience mortified because my feet were dirty. "Dying, and with dirty feet. Well, really!"

I got my first newspaper review for *The King and I*. Ian had told the reporter from the *Willesden and Brent Chronicle* words to the effect that "Jonathan Veira – whatever it is that makes a performance worth watching, he has it." I filed the press cutting away and, strangely, somebody sent me a copy of the picture and article the other day. Me with hair! It reminded me of how far I have come since those days. Thankfully, the reviews have, essentially, remained more or less positive over the past thirty-four years.

For much of this I have to thank my beginnings with a man who believed in what I did and who I was. Thanks, Ian.

CHAPTER 3

Learning the Ropes

Striving for success without hard work is like
trying to harvest where you haven't planted.

DAVID BLY

Some time ago I had the great pleasure of singing one of my favourite operas and one of the great *buffo* (comic) roles in my repertoire – the quack doctor selling the Elixir of Love (Dulcamara in *L'Elisir d'Amore* by Donizetti). It is a great opera with great tunes and I love doing it. This time it was in Leipzig, Germany. The Germans do love to laugh (whatever you may have heard), and maybe this city more than most. This is where the terrifying Stasi, the East German secret police, once reigned supreme and where the movement to German reunification began, in a church not far from the theatre.

I arrived at the opera house with no knowledge of the director apart from the fact that he was French. As is customary at the beginning of a rehearsal period, we all gathered together in the theatre to talk through the director's concept for this production. After explaining how it would all run, he turned to me and said:

"Monsieur Veira, norm-a-lee you would come on from ze side of ze stayge. *Oui?*"

I said, "*Oui.*"

"And norm-a-lee you would come to ze centre of ze stayge. *Oui?*"

"*Oui.*"

"Zen you would go forward to ze front of ze stayge and sing ze aria. *Oui?*"

"*Oui.*"

"Zen, ze public would go *absolutement* wild. *Oui?*"

"*Oui*," I said, humbly.

"Well, Monsieur Veira, I was theen-king we could do somezing totally diff-er-ent. *Oui?*"

"*Non!*" (I wanted to cry in response). What I actually said was, "What exactly do you mean, Monsieur?" At which point he produced a body harness and pointed to the top of the theatre.

"Well, Monsieur Veira, I was theen-king we could flyeeee you in!" he pronounced enthusiastically, demonstrating with his hands how I would float gracefully about fifty feet above the stage!

I gazed up in disbelief. What had I let myself in for? Would I get out of this alive? How was I going to sing a fiendishly difficult aria and fly at the same time? But the director had a gentle insistence that this was an integral part of his concept and design for this production of *L'Elisir d'Amore* in Leipzig. I was to be a mere cog in the machinery that brought this to fruition. Thanks a lot, I thought.

When the time came, I climbed into the harness and the stage crew tightened every strap and buckle until I was trussed up like a chicken! I stood there feeling extraordinarily uncomfortable (gentlemen will understand what I mean) and bemused. Was this really going to happen? Clearly it was, as two wires were lowered from the "flies" above the stage and clipped onto the shoulders of my harness. The safety protocols were obviously followed rigorously and I don't have a problem with heights, but to say I was terrified would be an understatement. My belief in a God who cares about me and who knows about every sparrow falling really kicked in! But the sparrow still falls, doesn't it – and what about a fat guy falling?

One final tug at all the straps, and the nice German technical director asked me:

"*Alles gut, ja?*"

"*Ja, danke. Alles gut,*" I lied, knowing that absolutely nothing was good about this. At which point he spoke into his walkie-talkie to the guy operating the hydraulic system which would yank me over fifty feet into the air (think bungie jumping in reverse!). Just one word in German:

"*Geh!*"

On this command (it seemed at superspeed), I was yanked up into the air to become a distant speck at the top of the theatre. Opera glasses would not be enough – a telescope would be more appropriate for the public to see me clearly. I can't quite tell you the level of excruciating pain I felt as the force of gravity acted on my substantial frame, willing it to return to terra firma. From the safety of the ground they shouted up at me again:

"*Alles gut, ja?*"

This time, in a high-pitched squeak, lying through my teeth, I replied: "*Ja, danke!*"

What was wrong with me? Why hadn't I become an estate agent like my dad wanted me to be? At least that job was as safe as houses! The other thought going through my head was, "How am I going to sing a six-and-a-half-minute aria up here?" It had been thirty seconds and already my body was crying out to be reinstated to its natural position. They eventually brought me down and the director enthused:

"Zis will work very well, Monsieur. I am liking zis a lot."

Rehearsals then continued with their customary ebb and flow, some days good and some days bad, but we practised in rehearsal rooms where the harness was not available. Days turned into weeks until we arrived at the dress rehearsal. This was called an "open dress" because this meant more or less a full, if non-paying, audience would be attending the rehearsal. An audience is particularly useful when you are doing comedy, as by the time you reach the end of the rehearsal period nobody in the production team is laughing at anything any more. It is difficult to judge where the laughs will come, if indeed they do.

This particular afternoon the show was running well. The soprano and tenor sang their beautiful duet before Dulcamara (me) made his grand entrance from the side of the "stayge", only this time with a twist!

I stood in the wings, the nice man tightening everywhere that should be tightened until I was rooted to the spot. He attached the two wires while I was going over and over in my head the first words I had to sing. Funnily enough, I am terrible at remembering words and always sit in the dressing room until the last moment looking at my music. This was no exception. Tonight the words were:

"Udite! Udite! Oh rustici." ("Listen! Listen! Oh rustics.")

I heard the whispered words: *"Alles gut, ja?"*

I sputtered out automatically, *"Ja, danke. Alles gut."*

Then came the command: *"GEH!"*

Up I went in the same terrifying rapid movement, ever upwards. Once at the top of the flies I awaited the crash of the A major chord from the orchestra – the cue to drag me out sideways across the stage into full view of the audience. I forgot to mention that I also had three-foot-long wooden wings attached to my arms that I was meant to be flapping as I flew in. What a way to earn a living!

I began to sing: *"Udite! Udite! Oh rustici."*

As I was singing this first line I became aware that my right wing (and arm) was moving slowly but inexorably from right to left. More words:

"Attenti, non fiatate!" ("Pay attention, don't breathe!")

The arm movement was now gathering speed. I was trying to maintain my head position forwards towards the audience so that at least I could be heard. I was thinking, "What's going on here?!"

By now it was quite clear that I was spinning slowly round! Despite my efforts, I was no longer facing the audience but facing the back of the stage and the turning was getting faster and faster. I was spinning round and round, completely out of control, and the audience was now apoplectic with laughter, with me, the true professional, singing my little socks off. It must have sounded like the Doppler effect. The orchestra started looking up to see what was going on and eventually they stopped playing as I stopped spinning one way... and started spinning back the other way! This produced even more hilarity and I thought it time to stop singing.

When I came to a final stop, I shouted out in English to a German audience at an Italian opera, "Mama! I'm flying!" – which of course raised a huge laugh from the audience, the orchestra and (I think) even the production team, although I wouldn't count on that.

Everything was reset and I restarted the aria from the beginning. All this because someone forgot to untangle the wires at the top of the theatre before attaching them to the Veira shoulders. The event was so hilarious that I was mentioned in the press the next day.

Two days later we opened the show for real. The nice man attached the wires.

"*Alles gut, ja?*"

"*Ja, danke. Alles gut.*"

"*Geh!*"

The A major chord came from the orchestra, and I was swung out over the stage. I dangled perfectly still, managing to sing the whole aria without any unwanted circular movement. However, I am sure I heard the collective sound of 1,200 disappointed Germans saying:

"Ooh – shame!"

So how did I go from a school production of *The King and I* to dangling fifty feet above a stage singing Italian to Germans?

Well, my parents bought me a bike.

My bike was a brand-new Peugeot 21-gear; it had 531 double-butted tubing with all the bits! It was a glorious machine and I rode that bike for three years all over London and Great Britain. Not a helmet to be seen and only one accident in all the time I owned it. I loved that bike and would give good money to have it back in my shed. It was freedom, independence and, let's face it, incredible for fitness. I would ride for a morning to see my sister Ruth in Maidenhead and then promptly ride back! Would the person who stole it please bring it back? It was a big deal to my parents, not just because it was hard earned, but because they knew I was going to use it to ride away from home. Mum has since told me that to see me getting on that bike was a sad day for her. I guess it was a sad day for me too, as I would never permanently live there again.

In the 1970s higher education was not by any means as broadly available as it is now. Then approximately only 10 per cent of the country went on to higher education. Now the figure is close to 48 per cent, though with government cuts and higher fees we may move to a reduction in those levels. For many families in Britain, the luxury of spending three years studying after leaving school was just not an option.

None of my family had ever been to university, so none of us had any real concept of what it was like or how to apply for a place there. We knew it was where people who got better paid, often more rewarding jobs went before entering the job market, but that was about it.

I got reasonable A Levels, nothing to set the world alight, but I did OK. Other than music, my experience at school had not greatly enhanced my desire to continue my education. All things considered, without a concerted effort from Ian the music teacher, who doubled as my guardian angel, I would have been far, far less motivated to apply for my step into another world, or in my case, Whitelands College, then part of the Roehampton Institute.

The University of Roehampton dates back to the 1840s, comprises four distinct colleges and is located in a tranquil oasis of green fields that you would never expect to find so close to the heart of London. Those colleges were among the first in the UK to admit women to their scholarly ranks. There were six women to every man admitted when I was there. Nice odds! Many of the fourteen staff then tutoring music at Roehampton had established international reputations for their work in an extensive range of disciplines. And discipline was what I got from Roehampton.

The study of music at Roehampton was conducted in the tradition of the Conservatoire – classical without augmentation from the worlds of jazz or other contemporary genres (except for a week here or there when a visiting lecturer would bring us Brubeck or Dylan).

I got my first lesson in discipline from a very fine lecturer called Richard Stangroom. He taught me conducting, both choral and orchestral. I had prepared to conduct a choral piece called *Rejoice in the Lamb* by Benjamin Britten. I had not prepared enough, however, and there I was with fifty singers and I could not make the piece work. Furthermore, I couldn't work out how to make it better. It was an incredibly difficult piece and technically beyond my reach at that time because of my lack of preparation.

You can't wing it with such a choir, all of whom are fellow music undergrads and looking to you for leadership. Conducting properly involves more than just understanding the notes on the page – you are guiding, directing the singers so that they can perform as the composer intended, to the best of their combined abilities. Richard Stangroom knew I was winging it and in no uncertain terms proceeded to teach me a lesson I have never forgotten. The highly edited and cleaned-up version goes like this:

"Don't you ever embarrass me like that again. Never turn up to anything musical that you are part of, ever, for the rest of your life as unprepared as this. Whatever you decide to do with music, whether you sing, conduct, write or play – learn from this."

Fortunately, this was not in front of the fifty singers, but I think he may have slammed a door at that point. However, I learned my lesson. Thanks, Richard – sadly no longer with us, and yet he is still with me at every point of preparing music; a great musician and a funny man.

Before we leave him, one occasion I remember well was at a performance of *The Dream of Gerontius* by Elgar that Richard was conducting. It was the University choir of 300 plus an enormous orchestra and it was 5.30 p.m. The concert was to begin at 7.00 p.m. Suddenly Richard ran across the church we were performing in to the gents' dressing area and said in a panicky voice, "I have left my dress trousers at home. I need a pair now!" To explain, he was five foot four and very slim. He borrowed the dress-suit trousers from a young man who was five foot ten, with a thirty-six-inch waist! By the beginning of the very first chorus, as usual, he became very animated, and out came the shirt and down slipped the trousers. He was left conducting with one hand, holding up the trousers with the other for most of the first half. The young man, meanwhile, was put at the back of the choir with Richard's fawn-coloured trousers on, flapping around his shins. Dear Richard.

Who said "An overnight success takes at least ten years"? Probably someone who wanted people to know that success in life is not all about finding the right get-rich-quick scheme or just a case of being born under a lucky star. Bruce Barton, the legendary advertising executive, once observed: "Most successful men have not achieved their distinction by having some new talent or opportunity presented to them. They have developed the opportunity that was at hand."

This is essentially what is wrong, in my view, with the *X Factor* road to fame and fortune. Microwave success; fast-food fodder. Success in anything is a hard road.

Working hard at what you want to get better at, day in, day out – making mistakes, failing, learning something and trying again. Any great achievement – the iPad 2.0, a cathedral, a concerto that still moves an audience 100 years on (and let's not forget my wonderful Dyson vacuum cleaner!) – all these things start with a decision to do the best you can with what you have. You simply start from where you are, take one faltering step, and then another. And then you fall down the stairs and get up again smiling, and off you go again (see my DVD *An Audience with JV*, for example).

Later on, when I was at the Opera Studio – a kind of finishing school for opera singers, if you will – I spent time with another influential Richard – Richard Van

Allan CBE. He was one Britain's most versatile operatic bass singers. He enjoyed a distinguished career with an enviable repertoire, performing often at Covent Garden and the English National Opera, as well as many of the significant international opera houses. Van Allen was a man who had great natural talent and much success in his chosen field; a singer recognized by many to embody "all the virtues that make the complete artist – vocal beauty and technique, musicianship, language, dramatic ability, stylistic authority" (*The Times*, 9 December 2008). He shared the secret to his success with me one rainy day at the Opera Studio:

"Right, Jonathan," he said. "I have three things to tell you that will be the most important pieces of advice you ever get about how to make a success of your career."

I was all ears and ready to take notes as he put a hand on my shoulder and delivered the wisdom gleaned from a long and successful career:

"Be on time, be on time and be on time."

That was it. Richard Van Allen was echoing the sharp but lucid words of Richard the First back at Roehampton. Talent will get you over the hill and round the bend, but what gets you over the finish line is discipline. Showing up, being completely present, not ever thinking that you deserve to be where you are or have learned all there is to learn; staying fresh and engaged.

Putting on a show, any show, is all about timing. Think about a movie set. If the director shows up late, if the catering manager is behind schedule with lunch, if Morgan Freeman is stuck on the phone to his mother, or Cameron Diaz's costume gets lost in transit, the movie will be delayed. The more people you have working on a show, the later things can get. Time is always money and lateness means stress – a little at first, but it quickly grows.

I have figured out that it is far better to be reliable and very good than unreliable and brilliant. You may not be the best actor or singer in the world, but if you are good enough at what you do and you show up on time, people will want to hire you again. I'm not the best singer in the world, I'm not the best performer. I am one of many very good people in my profession who make a living from what we do. In interviews people often ask me who, in my opinion, is the best singer in the world. It is essentially a flawed question. How can there be just one best singer in the world? Our profession is not like this. There are hundreds, if not thousands, of highly talented and gifted performers, both nationally and internationally, that I could name and rank among the best I know. But on any given day one might outshine the other for various reasons.

A casting director only has to have one show stumble or fail because of the antics of an unreliable but brilliant performer to vow only ever to hire people who can get the job done – people who show up on time, ready to work.

It's not that difficult. If you are chasing around trying to find your principal singer or making calls to find out what happened to your chief lighting technician, you have to take your eye off all the other balls you are juggling. Think about how many balls you would have in the air if you were putting on an opera – cast, orchestra, venue, staging, lighting, catering, transport, marketing, press, rehearsals, first night, reviews. The clock is ticking, the money meter is humming. An opera works like a clock: the sum of the whole is only ever going to be as good as the individual parts.

If the curtain does not go up on time, or your much-hyped star fails to make the stage, the blame will not always be apportioned fairly or in due measure. When you are putting on a show, there is nowhere to hide. Every little detail is out there, on show. Every little helps, every person matters. The lady who makes tea, the man who cleans the theatre after everyone else goes home, the music student who shows people to their seats or sells ice-cream at the interval, the fire officer who makes sure the exits are clear, the scene changers and costume makers, the personal assistant who books the flights, the girl who gets the singers from their dressing rooms to the stage on time. Vital ingredients one and all. We all bring what we bring to the party, something I have recognized after a quarter of a century of being in the business and also of being part of a church. It is the same principle – we all have different things to contribute to make up the whole. So now, when I am part of a show, I remember that everyone has a vital role to play in helping it to happen and for the show to go on.

The two Richards, among others, helped me to develop the mindset of a professional entertainer. In whatever capacity, the show must go on, regardless of my personal circumstances. For example, I was performing in Lyon and on the opening day of the opera I had a phone call from Sue to say that her father had died at one o'clock that morning. There was little I could do and though the opera company had sympathy with me, they required and expected me to perform that night. I was personally devastated by his death and for the feelings that I knew my family would be experiencing without me, but I had a duty to and respect for the audience who had paid to see this performance. I always want to make sure that my audiences go home rewarded.

Duty seems to be a very old-fashioned virtue. Duty to each other and duty to society in general. We are responsible for each other – very much like bees in a hive (as J. B. Priestly observed in *An Inspector Calls*). That notion made a huge impression on me as a child and it seemed that people I came into contact with re-emphasized the notion. Maybe I'm wrong, but I sense that people are slightly embarrassed when others talk of duty, yet it is one virtue that I cling to and try to live by. However, it must be said that duty can lead us to agree to dangle fifty feet above a stage. That and, of course, a substantial fee!

CHAPTER 4

Which Way to Go?

*Whether you turn to the right or to the left, your
ears will hear a voice behind you, saying, "This is
the way; walk in it."*

ISAIAH 30:21 NIV

Backstage can be a very dangerous place
to be. It is often pitch dark and as I can't
see particularly well without my glasses,
it's not always an easy place for me to be. Let's face it,
it is a major health hazard and it is why such major
precautions are taken on stage at all levels. Scenery falls
from the "flies", as happened at Wexford Festival Opera
in the middle of a live radio broadcast. Doors on stage
move and open in weird and wonderful ways and people
can fall into orchestra pits! Surely not, I hear you say,
but that is absolutely what I managed to do in 1987 at
Glyndebourne Festival Opera during rehearsals for that
wonderfully titled opera, *The Electrification of the Soviet
Union* by Nigel Osbourne.

I was standing on the stage, about to begin part of

73

the music. I stepped forward to speak to the conductor, David Gowland, and stepped unusually far forward onto the front apron of the stage. All I remember is the feeling of nothing beneath my feet and dropping straight down into the orchestra pit. What I hadn't realized was that they had covered up the front of the stage with netting to protect the members of the orchestra from water that had been thrown earlier during the rehearsals. Fortunately for me, and them, the orchestra pit was empty, and this was the only time I have ever hit a top B flat! People at Glyndebourne still remember the terrifying sound as I landed full square onto what should have been the second violins!

I remember lying there thinking, "Well, that's that, then. Probably broken my back or neck, so I shall be the first Chief Ironside of opera."

"Stay still!... Don't move!... Keep quiet!" came the cries. They had called the ambulance and very soon I was being immobilized and whisked off to Eastbourne General Hospital. This was in the days before mobile phones, but someone found me an old portable phone which took ten-pence pieces. Sue picked up the phone and my first words to her were: "Don't worry. I'm fine. But I am in Eastbourne General Hospital!"

Very comforting for her, especially as she was three weeks away from giving birth to our first son. I was in perfect control of the situation and chatting enthusiastically to the staff. The registrar was planning to give me something to calm me down when the director of the opera house, who had come with me, said, "No, don't worry, he's always like that!"

Fortunately for me (and them), I hadn't broken anything, but was severely bruised. The hospital staff offered me the helpful suggestion that I stay away from stages!

Not only is the stage a dangerous place to be, but a perplexing place too, at times. Try being in a country where the instructions to come to the stage for your moments are conducted in a language you don't speak – Danish, for example! The stage managers and crew were all excellent, but on this particular night I hadn't been paying attention. Suddenly, over the tannoy in my dressing room I heard a frantic call for "Jonathan Veira to come to the stage", this time in English. Somehow, I had missed the call to my next entry. At the end of the soprano's aria I was meant to be twelve feet above the stage, ready to lean out of a makeshift window. The aria duly finished, with me still in my dressing room, roughly forty seconds from the top of the stairs! A stage-hand, sensing the growing agitation of the beautiful principal singer who was waiting for my window to open, banged hard on my door. I raced to the stage, colliding with all manner of people and objects along the way.

I flung the door open, dressed scantily in a pair of long johns, and gasped my way through my lines. Suave.

There are always people everywhere backstage, usually about eighteen of them, waiting to move enormous chunks of scenery or get something that someone has forgotten. At the next performance, not wanting to be late again, I left my dressing room early. There was a crowd of stage-hands jostling around my door pretending to block my way, and then I saw them. All eighteen of the backstage crew were waiting with torches, forming an escort, lining my way to the stage. As I went past they all patted me on the back saying, "Hey Jonathan, today you can see where you are going! You won't miss it this time."

I was vaguely amused at the time but looking back, I realize that it was the technical crew's way of looking after me. I did not speak much Danish, but every night at the end of the show, I made a point of thanking the crew for their work. If you ever need to do the same while you are in Denmark, the words you will need are: *"Tak for i aften, tak for i aften."* ("Thank you for this evening, thank you for tonight.")

If anything went wrong, they were always there for me. A few words, like a simple gesture, can make a genuinely strong connection. At the end of the tour the technical crew all showed up in T-shirts that said, "Jonathan Veira Crew, Royal Theatre Denmark" on the back. I was very touched.

Whatever country I am in, I thank the crew every night for all their help and work *in their language*. I will always be grateful to those guys in Denmark for showing me the way to go. Way to go, guys!

Although I spent much of my childhood playing the piano, in the early days at Roehampton I was known as a viola player. The viola gets a bad rap among the heady pantheon of more revered orchestral instruments. Not only that, but the viola player is assumed to be fairly stupid. They get the filler parts, like an extra in a crowd scene. Frustrated with the lack of interesting parts to test my skills, I walked into a shop and said with a flourish, "My good man, I'd like to buy a flute, please!"

The man looked at me knowingly and after a small pause said, "You're a viola player, aren't you?"

"How did you know?" I replied, astonished at his prescience.

"Well, first of all, this is a fish-and-chip shop…"

Joking aside, it was time to make some decisions, as I was now faced with the stark choice that every student faces: what to specialize in. For me it was not so much an academic choice as a musical one. I had to decide between conducting, piano, viola or singing.

There are days in our lives, significant days, when we reach these decisive points. Maybe not today, but an inevitable sometime. I chose to lay my viola down, push the piano a little further away and concentrate on singing.

My singing tutor was a lady named Susan Gray. I remember the first day I met her – partly because I was wearing a natty pair of Levi 501s. Now I wear Levi 747s! (I just had to get that joke in.)

The first thing Susan asked me to do was to sing a

scale. Simple, you might think, for someone who knows how scales work. Not exactly. I mean, how do you sing a scale for someone whom you are trying to convince that you are serious about the study of singing? Someone, to boot, who actually knows what a sung scale should sound like?

At the time I was working my way through university by singing covers of Billy Joel and Elton John songs at the impressively French-sounding restaurant Le Grand Café on Battersea Rise. A little piano tucked into the corner, about £15 a night and all the burgers you could eat. I soon discovered that the best way to sing covers, the way guaranteed to get your audience on side, was to sound like the original artist. I got very good at working out the intonation, the accents, the vocal "keys" to becoming Stevie Wonder, Ray Charles or Stevie Winwood.

When presented with this momentous challenge, however – how to sing a scale to impress your brand-new tutor – I immediately deferred to what I knew best. I thought I had better sing my scale like somebody who would know how to sing a scale – an opera singer. By this point I had been to the sum total of one performance by the English National Opera in 1974, *The Flying Dutchman*, with Sir Norman Bailey. I gathered up all this non-extensive knowledge, plus a few enhancements gleaned from BBC Radio 3, and sang that scale copying what I thought an opera singer sounded like. I was back to my "fitting in" mode.

Then Susan asked me to sing it again, and I

practised singing scales for half an hour. After that she went home, me none the wiser. I later found out that she told her husband, over a cup of tea, that she had "found" her international opera singer – but that it was no use because I was too lazy, couldn't take it seriously and would never put the work in. She had spotted something in my voice that she felt she could develop with me, but feared that my tendency to play the fool might dilute the process! From that day on, despite her misgivings, Susan nurtured me, giving me Italian songs to work on, songs to develop my vocal ability. Little did I know that vocal chords take a good long time to come into their own. It is only now, having reached my fiftieth birthday (only *very* recently, mind you), that I am at the peak of my powers as a bass baritone. For years I was known as a "baby" vocally. From age thirty-five onwards you start coming into your own as a bass baritone.

Funnily enough, years later, I met Sir Norman Bailey (as I said, the first opera singer I heard) when we worked together on *The Bartered Bride* at Glyndebourne. I was singing one of the leading roles, Kecal, in Czech, and he was playing the part the father. I told him that I had seen him in *The Flying Dutchman*.

"Did you enjoy it?" he asked.

"No!" I said with conviction. "I hated it and thought if there is one thing I will never do, I will *never* sing opera."

At which point he burst out laughing. Another truly lovely man and a great artist, to boot.

Meanwhile, back at Le Grand Café, I was developing a bit of a following. I had become the musical favourite of Le Grand's coterie of very camp waiters who, along with their friends, decided to take me under their wing. Whenever I would play, people would ask for requests – a scribbled note along with a 50p or a £1 note (!) saying things like, "Please can you play 'You Make Me Feel Like a Natural Woman'. Thank you, Talisha xxxx."

One night, the wine was flowing and a man, well-dressed and swaying slightly, came over to the piano. He put £10 in the jar where the regulars would drop their requests along with a 50p piece. I was amazed at him giving me such a huge "tip". Ten pounds then was like £50 now and represented three quarters of my entire gig fee for the evening. Then a waiter scurried over:

"Do you know who that was?" he stage whispered.

I had no idea who the well-dressed man with the slight accent was.

"He's a real-life Count and he just *bought* you for the evening!" The waiter fixed me with a dramatic stare.

I finished my set, got on my small motorcycle and fled as fast as a Honda 70 could flee.

My small but perfectly formed Honda 70 got me out of trouble on more than one occasion. That was, until it blew up.

I loved that motorbike. It cost me £50 and a gallon of petrol would last much longer than it should have. We were a great team. Unstoppable. Until that fateful day when I started up my beloved bike and the revs just got higher and higher. There was nothing I could do to stop it. Somebody somewhere helpfully shouted, like they do in movies, "Get out! Get out! She's gonna blow!"

And, like they do in movies, I jumped over a wall and waited – then KABOOM! My much-loved bike had revved itself into oblivion. I put what was left of it in the paper and sold the spares for more than I paid for it. I'm not sure to this day how that happened. The next bike I bought got stolen while I was otherwise occupied with my girlfriend, now wife, Sue. I was able to claim for it on my insurance until the police found it two years later and I had to give the money back.

Which brings us to Sue. In the days before the Honda 70, I turned up at a house in Clapham for a band rehearsal and leaned my pushbike against a handy wall, all out of puff and in need of oxygen and a foil blanket. Sue opened the door. She says she was taken with my gorgeous pumped, bronze arms. I was simply taken with her absolute gorgeousness. I was also wondering what a classy girl like her was doing anywhere near our band rehearsal.

Sue remembers thinking I was a bundle of nervous energy. My nerves always had kittens when I had to meet new people. I found the whole process terrifying. I was fine in a social situation as long as I was playing the piano or guitar – a barrier between me and an actual conversation. But meeting people, especially women, was difficult, verging on impossible.

Through some kind of miracle, I had a girlfriend

when I met Sue, so other than thinking, as any man would, that she was gorgeous, that was it. But something about Sue calmed me. I felt at peace around her and we became friends. Me, nervy and nineteen; she, way out of my league.

Sue had completed her undergraduate studies in Biochemistry at Manchester University. She joined the Civil Service and was on their fast track, tipped for the top. Meanwhile, she and I were getting closer and closer and she would frequently lend a listening (and, might I say, sisterly at this point) ear and an appropriate Art Garfunkel record.

When we were not trying to work out the vagaries of life and love, as a complete counterpoint to all the student angst we would visit a local Borstal. A Borstal was another seventies social experiment – a type of youth prison in the United Kingdom run by the Prison Service and intended to reform serious young offenders.

Sue and I used to visit the boys in our local Borstal in Feltham as part of the prison ministry of Laleham Parish Church. We visited for years to talk to the boys, sing to them, and talk about the faith that helped us make sense of all the brokenness in our world. Sue says that after many visits there, I was doing a concert and speaking when quite suddenly, she realized she loved me! Interesting – falling in love when in a penal institution! I would much rather have told you that she fell in love with me after listening to me serenading her with a current love song; but no, penal institution it was.

Just after this realization on Sue's part, we went to a party in Clapham where Sue twisted her ankle (she claimed). I sat on the floor stroking her foot. It was late. If Cinderella had been at this party she would have been driving home in a pumpkin. I helped Sue to her carriage – a tiny Mini (her Mini, I might add) – and she managed to drive me back to my college flat, as I couldn't drive then. The Uni gates were locked, so before I attempted to scale an eighteen-foot wall (my only way back in) by standing on the Mini, I kissed her. Maybe I thought I would fall off the wall and never get the chance again. It was a beautiful thing. However, the dent in the Mini remained until we sold it some years later.

Now we have been married for twenty-nine years and have known each other for thirty-one. It was quite some kiss. I would never be who I am today, or have been able to achieve the things I have, without Sue. I looked at her this morning and honestly, I still can't work out how I got this girl to marry me. She is still out of my league.

In between conducting, singing, running away from a Count and courting Sue, my mate Mark and I had formed a band. Two girl singers, one guitar, one piano. There was some universal law of the seventies that all British Christian bands had to be called something clever. It was either a meaningful Greek word or had to have "cross" in the title: "Cross [insert appropriate other word here]". So you would get bands like Zoe, Agape and Logos, along with the inevitable Crossways, Crosstalk… you get the idea. For some reason known only to the universal law of the seventies, we decided to call ourselves Crossword. It wasn't the most memorable or cool name; more afternoon tea in the sun lounge than Velvet Underground. In fact, apparently it was such an unmemorable name that people would introduce us as Crossroads or Crosseyed or any other word association that came to mind.

I had found a fantastic Greek word that meant "seed". It was very biblical. Remember the story of the farmer who went out to sow his seed, and some landed on stony ground, some on fertile land, and so on? The Greek word used here for "seed" is *spermitoss*. I could just see the poster on the church notice-board:

> *An evening with Spermitoss, 7–11 p.m. A great night out for all!*

I thought it was brilliant, but there were just so many ways it could have gone wrong. I am certain it would have been better than being called Crossword, although we might perhaps have been booked into more alternative venues than church halls and coffee bars.

We did all manner of gigs, including something called Royal Week. This is not the week the Queen sets aside every year to listen to British Christian bands, but rather an offshoot of the annual Spring Harvest festival. After our gig, a man came up to us with a rapturous look on his face.

"You were wonderful! I have been to everything

else here and you are the best. Great singers, wonderful, wonderful!"

I thought he was going to burst into a Frank Loesser show tune until I spotted that he had not one but *two* hearing aids. "No wonder he thinks we're good," said the ever-encouraging voice in my head.

We made such an impression on this man, who turned out to be an RAF chaplain, that he invited us to perform at RAF Henlow, a base sandwiched between Bedford and Luton, fairly near to London, but a very long way when your only transport is a Mini.

It is fair to say that we arrived at the base feeling nearer dead than alive. A Friday evening along the A40, four of us plus two big guitars, an amplifier and whatever other paraphernalia we required, all squashed in Sue's Mini 850. I hate arriving late for a gig and this night we were late. We got to the RAF base just before our slot and in time to catch the tail end of a performance by the Henlow bell ringers. They might as well have been ringing warning bells.

Here is some free advice: never take a gig that you have well-founded reservations about. I had mixed feelings about our appearance that night, warning bells that got louder as my band-mate Mark decided that now was the perfect time to restring the guitar that I, not he, was due to play – just before we were due to go on. And go on we did, launching into a folk-rock version of "Oh Sinner Man" in the key of E.

I wanted to run and hide. All I could hear was wrong

notes as I discovered with horror that not one blessed string on my newly restrung guitar was in tune. As all good guitar players do, I accomplished some makeshift tuning while pretending to play – at least I got the bottom E string tuned for that song. I stood there like a good viola player, keeping time on my one string. I remember giving Mark my best withering stare. Maybe it was a revenge attack for something I had done earlier.

All that would redeem the evening now was a hard-earned supper. When you are someone like Mariah Carey and you turn up to perform at the O2 Arena or even *Strictly Come Dancing*, you get what is known in the music business as a "rider". A rider consists of little comforts requested by the world-weary entertainer to make them feel at home, loved, cared for, appreciated. Welcome gifts, if you will. Mariah Carey's rider may have requests like:

"Miss Mariah Carey requests only white tulips and eight Jo Malone Pomegranate Noir candles in her dressing room. She must have two packets of Skittles in a silver bowl with all the blue ones removed. Oh, and a three-month-old Chihuahua in a pen for the interval, please."

Our rider went something like this:

RAF Henlow: "What do you want to eat after the show?"

Us: "Fish and chips, please."

RAF Henlow: "OK."

After our long ordeal, we were ravenous. Sue had

driven to the gig straight from work, I from a full day at Uni. We were anticipating piping-hot fish and chips with a touch of vinegar and properly salted. However, someone at RAF Henlow had decided to buy our supper at 5.00 p.m. By this time it was 9.30 p.m.

"We kept them wrapped up for you," our host said brightly.

Unwrapped, stone cold, it was not a great end to a difficult evening. The RAF chaplain's enthusiasm for our musical talent remained undimmed – so much warmer than our supper.

"You were fantastic, fantastic! Sorry about the fish and chips!"

And that was Crossword. If only we had been called Spermitoss – how different life could have been.

CHAPTER 5

A Whole New World

Nothing is certain but uncertainty.

LATIN PROVERB

Sometimes in life, we get to live our dreams. At other times, things happen that are more akin to your deepest fears or worst nightmares. I feel like the guy at the beginning of the TV show *The Twilight Zone*, introducing a horror story.

Many years ago I had the great pleasure of going to the Caribbean island of Barbados. I had been invited as a guest of the Barbados Festival – a celebration of the arts, both high and low, and everything in between. From opera to theatre to steel bands, it had everything. Barbados is quite simply a beautiful island and, on hearing about the invitation, my wife said:

"No doubt you are going to go on your own on this one, leaving me to look after the kids?"

"It's a tough job, but someone has to do it!" I said cheerily.

The job was to perform in a new opera by Stewart

Copeland, the drummer from the band The Police. His musical heritage stretched back to that other famous Copeland, Aaron Copeland, and so he had a desire to write for the classically trained voice. The other attraction for him was that he played polo and John Kidd, who ran the festival at that time, was a keen polo player.

So, all was set fine. The opera, *The Cask of Amontillado*, was a dark tale from Edgar Alan Poe of a man being bricked up and left to die. I arrived in Barbados and it was just as I had remembered it. Beautiful, warm and with those lovely cicadas singing at night-time. As I arrived at the hotel, the sun was setting over the palm trees right on the beach. As I said, "A tough job..."

We were to rehearse for approximately three hours a day and then do two performances at the end. The rehearsals were haphazard but interesting, as they would often be in the back gardens of once famous but now obscure film stars from the golden Hollywood days. As with any new piece, we had to find our way quickly into the bits that would work and the bits that wouldn't. The set consisted of basically one door and some bricks, but we had to have it made on the island. Easier said than done in a place where the phrase *mañana* covers just about everything! Everything happens at a much slower pace because of the heat and it gets dark suddenly at around 6.00 p.m. every night. Therefore, if it isn't done in the morning, pretty much it isn't done at all.

Around the beginning of week two, I got a phone call from my agent, Helen Sykes:

"Jonathan, Covent Garden desperately need an understudy for an opera in rehearsals now. It's called *Gawain and the Green Knight* by Harrison Birtwhistle."

The understudy had had to pull out and they needed someone to take his place. Could I do it? The opera opened on the Thursday after I returned from Barbados on the Monday.

"No, of course not."

I hadn't seen it and I couldn't possibly agree to do something I hadn't seen, and the timescale was stupid… blah blah blah. There were numerous reasons why I couldn't. There was also a friend, a staff director at Covent Garden, who was there with me in Barbados, who counselled me not to do the job. A no-brainer, I thought, and left it at that. Some two hours later, interrupting my sunbathing, Helen phoned back. This time emphasizing the fact that they really, *really* needed me, as it was a hugely difficult role and no one else they knew could even get near to attempting it. It was covering the role that the famous bass, John Tomlinson, was singing. She said also that they were willing to pay me what was silly money as far as I was concerned, to have me as the insurance cover. She also assured me at that point that they thought it was highly unlikely that I would ever have to sing it, as John Tomlinson would never cancel; he was rock solid. She told me that as the show was opening just days after I got back and as I would not have any time to look at the score, I would not have to attend any rehearsals for understudies.

"OK, Helen," I said, "could you get them to fax me some pages of the music to my hotel?" I thought I should at least look at the music.

Very early the next morning there was a loud banging on my bedroom door. I opened it to the irate and huge Barbadian woman who ran the hotel.

"You tell all your friends to stop faxing me!" she demanded. "I have completely run out of fax paper. Thirty-eight pages!" She threw them on the floor and departed angrily.

Judging from the fax, this was a machine bought around 1914. The old photographic-type paper was slightly slimy to the touch. I spent the next two hours with a pair of scissors cutting the paper, turning it over and over, trying to make out which was the top and which was the bottom of the music.

This is twentieth-century music and is therefore incredibly – and let me say this again, *incredibly* – difficult to read, sing and play. I phoned Helen back later that morning and expressed my fears but... Sue and I were tight for money in those days. Good old-fashioned greed took the place of good sense, and I agreed to do the job.

Skip to Monday at approximately 2 p.m. I arrived at London Gatwick and proceeded to the Opera House, Covent Garden, where the rehearsals were still going on. Everybody greeted me and I listened to various parts of the opera. It was inscrutable, certainly without a score, and I immediately had the thought in my head, "What have I done?!" John Tomlinson saw me and greeted me with the comforting words:

"It took me six months to learn this, but don't worry, you'll be fine."

Similarly comforting were Garry Howarth, the conductor and Mark Packwood, one of the pianists. Mark said, "I have half an hour. Shall we go and have a look at some of the music?" So I dutifully collected the scores from the librarian who bade me farewell with the words, "Good luck!"

We sat together at the piano for thirty minutes and got through three pages of music. It was impossible. I tucked the scores under my arm and made my weary way home. The show would open within two days and I was to do no more rehearsals. I looked at the music as best I could, but eventually closed the scores and put them on top of the piano.

The performances began and all went well, with rave reviews and no problems for me. Covent Garden were so confident that John would not fall by the wayside that they agreed to give me an N/A (non-availability, basically a day off) for one of the performances. This allowed me to do one of my one-man shows near Plymouth that had been set up by an old university friend, Ian Hiscock, who was working at a school down there. He had been planning this for a while and had sold many hundreds of tickets.

On the fateful day I made my way down to Plymouth. Half an hour away from the venue my car phone rang (at that time, mobile phones were the size of a small cottage). I answered: it was Sue. She spoke in a flat, controlled voice:

"Pull the car over. Pull the car over *now*."

I thought someone had died, at the very least. But it was a whole lot worse.

"You're on," she said. "You're on at Covent Garden tonight. You have to turn the car around right away and make your way via Guildford to pick up the score and your black tie. They want you to stand at the side of the stage and sing the part."

I had just driven for four and a half hours, and to get back would take at least five. It was approximately 1 p.m. and the show started, earlier than most, at 7 p.m., since it was a very long show. I remember thinking weakly, "This is it. This is the end of my career."

I had agreed to do this and there was no way I could sing any of it with any degree of accuracy, even while holding the music and looking right at the conductor. I had looked at just three pages in thirty minutes. The words, "You will never have to go on" were ringing in my ears. But suddenly, John was off – I still didn't know why – and my name was on the contract. I was the one who had agreed to do it and the responsibility was solely mine. What had I done? I thought it would be easier to drive into the central reservation and lose a couple of limbs. I was heading back on the M5 when my agent rang and I expressed my fears in no uncertain terms.

"You'll be fine," she replied confidently.

"You'll be fine"?! What was she talking about? This

was the end, as far as I could see – no way back. "You can't bluff your way out of this one, boy," I said to myself. This was going to be a headlong crash into disaster in front of a couple of thousand people and a management who had trusted me.

I arrived at home at about 5.15 p.m., by now a total wreck. I could barely speak. Sue could barely talk to me either and had little to say. She just handed me the music, the three big, thick, green scores full of music that I didn't know and had very little chance of speaking, let alone singing. Then she handed me my suit.

"You'll be needing this," she said bleakly.

I left and made my way to London, arriving at about 6.30 p.m. I remember parking illegally on double yellow lines in Floral Street, right next to the stage door, but not caring. I went in and there was Stella, the lovely stage manager who had always been so kind to me.

"Ah Jonathan, I'm so glad you're here!"

"Yes," I answered in a high-pitched squeak. I was in a stupor of fear – flight or fight. I made my way to the executioner's block. It was just a matter of time before the axe fell. This was the nightmare I had experienced in my dreams many times before, only this time it was happening for real, and I wasn't waking up.

Stella then said, "Now, Jonathan, the thing is, John would like to see if he can go on, if that's OK with you?"

"That's fine," I said, my voice a long way away. "That's fine."

John had been involved in a serious car accident

on the way back from Leeds and was believed to be in shock, so the doctor felt that he might go blank at any time. John, being a true professional, was keen to go on, so the management therefore decided that I should be ready in the wings. If John went blank, then I was to step out from the side of the curtain and keep the curtain up by singing.

"Oh," I said, still in the same far-away high-pitched voice.

They positioned me on stage right, just behind the curtain, with Mark Packwood, the pianist, serving as a relay conductor (i.e. relaying the beat to me). At some point, as the performance began and I stood there, literally losing weight on the spot, he turned to me and said:

"Oh! He *is* looking a bit peaky, isn't he?"

I could have killed him there and then, but only just had enough energy to breathe.

To cut a long story very short, the first half finished and John had stayed on. I asked if I could leave at that point, as he seemed to be secure and I felt on the point of collapse myself. To which they replied:

"No, we would like you to sit in the box above the stage and if he should stop singing, we will turn the spotlight on you to continue."

"Thanks," I said, in my now customary high-pitched voice.

Suffice it to say, John managed to survive until the end of the show and I closed the score with a mixed sense of utter relief and total breakdown. One of the management came and said to me:

"Jonathan, thank you so much for doing what you have done tonight – we really appreciate it. I suppose it's a good time to tell you now that the show was being taken by Radio 3 for future broadcast."

"Oh, good," I smiled wanly up at him.

I left the theatre that night, half the man that I was before. On arriving home, I went straight to the piano with the score in my hot little hands. Basically, I couldn't sleep for two days until I had come to grips in some way with the score and could, if asked, do something to find my way through a performance, should the occasion arise again.

The lesson here is: don't do it for the money; it really isn't worth it!

Daily life may seem like a series of stops and starts, the mundane merging with the occasional moment of drama. It is only when you get to look back, especially when you move into your forties, that you can see that the stops and starts belong to a journey. You start to see the tracks curving backwards rather than simply the stations along the way.

Some people plot a course through life entirely on their own. Me, not so much. When I look back now, I can see that there were key moments when, like a train that travels where the track wills, I was being guided along paths I might not otherwise have chosen. This guidance came in the form of significant people who not only stood up for me, but also gave me a gentle and, at times, insistent nudge in the right direction.

Like Mark, my erstwhile fellow Crossword member. Mark was a year or two older than me and I looked up to him. And while it seemed like everyone else was urging me to pursue a career as a gospel singer, dear old Mark kept telling me that the wise move would be towards opera.

It is thanks to Mark and others like him that I began to contemplate a career in opera – that I had the courage to take the first faltering steps in that direction. Now, any gospel singing that I do is informed by the discipline of opera, but if I had not been nudged along the way, I might never have touched anything but the furthest fringes of a world that has been my best teacher and sternest master.

I may have been on the verge of a whole new world, but on leaving Roehampton I was under the distinct impression that I had been left behind. That old graduate dilemma – "Now I need to get a job in the real world" – presented itself with a vengeance. My impression was that the real world did not seem to be crying out for music graduates.

As any performer will tell you, in the event that you are not able to do what you love, you do what you can. I really enjoyed working with children. I often ran play schemes through the summer, so I took a job I knew I could do at a children's nursery. No man had ever worked there and it took my obvious desperation and a lot of persuasion before they would agree to take me on. The boys and I got along famously, so the mothers and the staff were happy; it was all good. (Of course, if I presented myself there today, there would be absolutely no chance of being employed at that nursery in Clapham. The amount of red tape does not permit an offer of employment one day and turning up for work on the next.)

Even better, Sue and I got married on 4 September 1982. As we settled into our new life, I had the perfect day job for a musician, four or five hours a day, leaving me free to continue with music in the evenings. That job lasted me over a year and got me through what could otherwise have been a miserable taste of unemployment.

I stopped gigging with Crossword at all manner of tents and halls a short time after RAF "Henlowgate", partly because I was being invited to play, arrange and direct music for various people, one of whom was the famously energetic British Christian singer-songwriter and worship leader, Graham Kendrick. For approximately two years I worked with Graham, travelling around the country in his big red Passat Estate with keyboard in tow, and had a great time getting a taste for life on the road. This is where, as a young man, I was introduced to playing in front of very large audiences – sometimes of 30,000 or more – and at Christian events like Spring Harvest, a mere 5,000! It taught me a lot about band dynamics, as I was playing with some great musicians – people like

Raul D'Oliviera (flugel horn), Chris Mitchell (trombone), Phil Crabbe (drums) and Neil Costello (guitar), all of whom I continue to record with to this day.

Friendships were forged as we stayed in the weirdest places in some very strange venues. One of these included sharing a bunk bed with Graham in the north-east of England in January in thick snow – something which I am sure Graham has tried to forget, as the temperature inside was surely lower than that outside! In those days we were paid £40 a gig, and the work was sporadic and was nowhere near enough for me to quit my day job with the kids. The life of a gigging musician is nothing if not varied.

I nearly forgot to include another drummer, Martin Neil. He was outrageous and he was the drummer everyone wanted. He was brilliant, with a touch of eccentricity. You would be counting a song in – One, Two, Three... and in the nanosecond that preceded "Four!" Martin would interject and ask:

"Erm, hang on mate, how does this one go again?"

Drummers have a lot of kit. It's different to loading a couple of guitars into a Mini. I once asked Martin to play drums for me at a gig in South London, for the Baptist church Sue and I were attending at the time, Bonneville Baptist Church on the South Circular Road. He assured me that he would be able to get his equipment there. In the event, his car broke down (a not unusual occurrence in those days for nearly all of us – in fact, I seem to remember that I used to phone the RAC to tell them I was leaving the house so that they would be forewarned!), so Martin turned up with no drum-kit and some cheery words to calm my fears:

"Don't worry, Jonathan – I've bought my sticks along."

Then he disappeared. No time at all later, he had assembled a kit out of fire extinguishers, chairs, upturned waste-bins, you name it, all with different sounds, and proceeded to make music with them. It was a night to remember!

Once again I was doing OK, all the time working my day job and playing nights, not making enough to become a full-time professional musician. The wheels were turning, but slowly.

On 29 October 1941, Winston Churchill, that English bulldog of a politician, was asked to speak at Harrow, to the pupils of that very famous public school. He is quoted as saying: "Never, ever, ever, ever, ever, ever, ever, give in. Never give in. Never give in. Never give in." Then he sat down. Either Churchill had had very little time to prepare this speech, or he wanted to impart something simple but vital to those bright young people. Since he wasn't known for being underprepared, my money's on the latter.

So here is another bit of great advice for anyone trying to make it as a musician, an actor or whatever creative profession takes your fancy. Keep at it and never stop learning. My singing teacher at Roehampton had been quietly nagging me to apply for a post-graduate course at Trinity College of Music. She wanted me to work with a specific voice tutor called Elizabeth Hawes. Being the dutiful scholar that I was and for want of a better idea, I auditioned.

To my utter amazement, Trinity College of Music offered me a place immediately. Upon learning that I was debating not taking the place because I had no idea how I was going to pay the fees, they offered me a generous scholarship. I had, by now, worked on a total of one opera while I was at Roehampton: Mozart's *Don Giovanni*, playing the part of Leporello, Don Giovanni's much put-upon manservant. However, this was a mere extract from Act 1; the opera lasts about three and a half hours!

In short, I had still racked up almost no practical operatic experience – two performances (if you include Gilbert and Sullivan's opera *Trial by Jury*) plus a few rehearsals, to be precise. But here I was, with a new tutor who had a gut feeling that I had what it took.

Working with Elizabeth Hawes, I felt a bit like a farm-horse that has been given the chance to become a show-jumper, if only it could develop the right muscles to get over those high fences. Elizabeth would say things like, "Jonathan, we are just waiting for your voice to come into its own. You are young, you just have to be patient, you are just a baby!"

One day she was working with me on technique, breathing, using my diaphragm, understanding how the voice travels forward – and something *clicked*. I could feel a change as real as when the night sky gives way to daylight. Finally, I understood what it was all about. I had jumped my first high fence.

Ever with an eye on trying to make a living and with my new-found voice in my bag, I was entered by Elizabeth for the Peter Pears competition. The prize was a serious amount of money for the early 1980s – a very tempting £1,000, tax free.

The only way to win any popular, fiercely contested competition is to put your butterflies in a box, walk through the door like you mean it and face the judges down. I don't mean you should stand and glare at them, but you have to face them with the confidence to believe you should be there and the courage to perform at your best. The world of classical music is daunting enough, without standing opposite people who eat and drink opera and song repertoire for breakfast waiting to eat you up for dessert.

As with all good competitions, there is a lot of waiting around on hard chairs, sizing up the competition. It's not the most relaxing environment. There were heats in the morning, a couple of singers representing each music college, and you had to perform not one but two songs. If you got through this bear-pit, you were propelled through to the final and the dubious reward of a thirty-minute recital. Imagine that! About ten specialist, highly technical classical songs. I worked for hours with my pianist, Linda, to get to the point where I knew those songs as well as my heartbeat. It was so great to walk into the room with her, not alone at all. We did the first song and people applauded; Peter Pears and his fellow judges seemed to like it, but there was no way of telling at that point. They were generally impassive, as is often the case in classical music; little show of emotion. Time sped up as it does when your heart rate accelerates and I was through to the final four, for the evening concert. Just one man and three women left.

Now you are not just waiting in any hall on a hard chair, you are anticipating your moment in front of the judges at the Grand Hall of the Royal Academy of Music, Britain's oldest degree-granting music school. The Academy was granted a Royal Charter by King George IV in 1830. All that history staring down impassively at you from those esteemed walls.

If your butterflies needed a box before, now is the time to upgrade to something bigger. My ever-loyal wife and sole supporter Sue was in the audience willing me on. My family had no idea about this part of my life; at that point it was just Sue and I, plus three people who wanted to win just as much as I did. I have made it a rule never to listen to anyone else's performance when I have to compete against them. It is not a decision rooted in arrogance, more protection from the voice that wants to point out how much better they are than me. If you can't kill the voice off, at least isolate it, working on the premise that fires cannot burn without oxygen. Three women, one man. The only thing I could think of to say was: "May the best man win!"

Brilliant Veira, foot in mouth a speciality. Then it was my turn, and time turned hyper again until another voice, louder than the one in my head, announced:

"The winner is... Jonathan Veira!"

Sorry, who? I thought they were talking about someone else. Then there were smiles, a big cheque, lots of photographs and hugging. I had gone from being Daddy Day-care, part-time musician, to "A young, promising baritone. The voice of the future."

Sue and I entered a state I can only describe as happy disbelief. Having decided to enter the Peter Pears competition, and with the enthusiasm and optimism so neatly captured in that old British expression, "In for a penny, in for a pound", a week later I had also been entered for the Anna Instone Memorial Award, which was a one-off competition for musicians and singers, sponsored by Capital Radio. This was a £3,000 award and was conducted at the prestigious Wigmore Hall in London. I sang a twenty-minute programme and, to my great shock and genuine amazement, beat my fellow contestants to first place. One week, and so far £4,000! I had also been placed second in an inter-collegiate English singers' and speakers' contest, which bagged another £250.

Sue and I sat and looked at our bank balance. It had gone from pretty much zero to £4,250. This was a shock to us and I thought, "Maybe I can do this after all." To give you an idea, this amount of money equalled more or less an average salary for one year at that time. In addition to this, we had a number of silver plaques to brighten up our mantelpiece and remind us that dreams do sometimes come true.

I was now having a series of golden moments when everything Sue and I had worked for, got up early in the morning for, stayed out late at night for, believed for, refused to give up on, and practised for all those countless hours, was starting to pay off.

In the world of music, good news has a way of snowballing. The English music press attend all the prestigious competitions looking for a good story. You win something, especially more than one thing, and you are going to get more than one review. That year, I got more than one much-appreciated review saying, in so many words, that by far the finest singer was a young baritone called Jonathan Veira. A few days later I got an invite to audition at Glyndebourne.

But before Glyndebourne I need to talk about Wexford, which is where my professional opera career started in 1984.

The Wexford Opera Festival takes place every year in the months of October and November in the appealing county town of Wexford, southeastern Ireland – an ancient settlement founded by the Vikings in about 800 AD. A long time after the Vikings had left, in November 1950, the thriving town was visited by Sir Compton Mackenzie, the founder of the magazine *The*

Gramophone. Mackenzie, an intelligent writer on music, was to give a lecture to the Wexford Opera Study Circle. Bemoaning the lack of opera in the area, the group were encouraged by Mackenzie's suggestion that they should use their Theatre Royal – a theatre that he deemed perfectly suited to the production of particular operas – to stage their own.

In 1984 I was invited to Wexford to play the small part of Erste Wächter (First Guard) and take part in the chorus. I stood on the stage for half an hour, waiting with a spear and another singing guard called Brindley Sherratt – a stunning bass who has become a substantial international artist and a great colleague with whom I have worked more than once through the years. Our stage direction went something like this:

"Guards One and Two stand either side of door (sing)."

One line, and that was it. Standing on stage with a spear and then in the chorus, it all felt foreign to me, somewhat daunting. I was not entirely sure what I was doing there, but something kept me rooted to the spot. In fact, I still remember the line I had to sing twenty-six years later!

It was in Wexford that I learned one of the many secret tricks of the theatre. You may or may not be aware of the practice of using a certain well-known sweet and sticky brown carbonated drink to help protect performers from slipping on the stage, especially when the stage is sloping. It is called "coking" the stage.

It is common stage practice in opera to give the audience a better view of the action by inclining the floor, known as a raked stage. This way, upstage is at a higher elevation than downstage. We get the term "upstaging" – used when a performer is ruthlessly drawing the audience's attention away from a fellow performer – from the practice of moving one performer to a higher position on the rake. The upstaged performer, who stays lower down, must literally turn his back to the audience to address the other cast member. Never a good look.

The raked stage at Wexford had duly been applied with the world's most requested carbonated drink so that it would be nice and tacky in time for the first performance of the season. The performers would be on the rake in slippery tights, no shoes, so it was a necessary precaution to ensure they stayed put.

A short time later, a local cleaning lady (I mentally called her "Nancy") dutifully arrived to clean the stage. She went about her work, duly arriving at the rake and, being a good cleaner, was mortified at the state of the floor. "What on earth is this?" she cried, promptly bustling about with a mop and bucket until she had cleaned all the offending sticky stuff off the floor. The performance was well under way when a group of unsuspecting performers in shiny tights took their places on the rake – or rather, *briefly* took their places on the rake. Everyone slid forward, hanging on to each other and any scenery they could find. You can imagine the rest.

Wexford is a lovely place for opera and has a great

fund of stories like this one. On my first visit there in 1984 I took lodgings with a dear lady, the far side of sixty, who exhibited some of the most eccentric behaviour I had ever encountered. She took pleasure in showing me the house and explaining the house rules. The bathroom had a tiny plastic shower attachment, a million miles away from a power shower, and there was never ever enough hot water to have more than a sprinkling each morning. She informed me:

"I am sure a man of your size will manage to keep himself clean with this. A bath is an extra £1."

On showing me the lounge, which I was allowed to use, but only after certain hours in the evening, she turned on the coal-effect light on the electric fire. The electric bar was never to be turned on as, "It costs far too much, Jona-tan."

The bedroom was, to say the least, intimidating. On one wall was the Pope. On another was the Virgin Mary and right by my pillow was Jesus and the Sacred Heart. To sleep, I often turned them around to face the wall.

When I came in late after a performance, my landlady would sometimes be sitting in the lounge with the coal-effect light on – no heating. This was in November – it was freezing! – and she would be cradling a bottle of vodka, giving me, a young innocent, the "glad" eye! I would feign extreme tiredness, making my way quickly up to the bedroom, locking myself in with the Pope et al. I loved her to bits, and she wept when I left.

Everything, it seemed, was done in the Festival to

fleece the visitors, performers or not. Transactions were all in cash, up front. Prices in the hotels would rocket overnight, as did the drinks in the local pubs, but the people in Wexford were always fantastic, friendly and incredibly open. One night in particular, I remember going to a small bar called Fina Kelly's for a taste of the famous Irish Guinness. It was a tiny bar, no bigger than an average-sized front room, and had not been decorated, according to the owner, since 1945. The interior bore this out, and there sat in the corner of this tiny bar a very old piano with piles of old sheet music. I made the mistake of playing a few notes on this beaten-up old instrument, whereupon the locals practically tied me to the stool and forced me to play there until 3 a.m.! We covered everything from "When Irish Eyes are Smiling" to "Danny Boy" and back again, all to the accompaniment of, "So what will you be having, then? All on the house, Jona-tan!"

It was another world where drinking hours seemed to go on forever, but they have an unrivalled heart for singing and entertainment. The Irish (Murphy on my father's side) part of me seemed to find its home. Good times!

Glyndebourne was known to be a hot-house for young talent. Everyone who performed there was gifted, hard-working and wanted to make it. Many of the people I joined in the chorus went on to become well-known soloists: Gerald Finley (bass baritone), Anna Steiger (mezzo soprano) and Alastair Miles (bass baritone), to name but a few. Everyone was hustling for a chance to be recognized, looking for a small part or an understudy role. You were invited to Glyndebourne to serve your apprenticeship, to see if you would learn to swim, or sink without trace.

I had been given my big break. Now was the time to prove myself. Only, by my estimation, I knew next to nothing. Apart from being in the chorus of *Carmen*, I also had a brief understudy part as the messenger in *La Traviata*:

> *A messenger arrives with a letter from a lady (sings).*

One line again. I received £5 every night the opera was performed and £10 if I went on as the understudy. We're talking big time here!

It was tough. The people, the schedule, the chorus, everything about it was tough. About a week into my first Glyndebourne, I was on the telephone to Sue telling her that I wanted nothing more than to come home. It was like being thrown in with the lions. All the lions were strutting their stuff, watching how the other lions ate people. It wasn't vicious per se, simply an all-consuming environment populated by ambitious, single-minded individuals who were working as hard as anyone could to make it, knowing that in reality, very few would.

You were constantly being watched, assessed, and

marked up or down – one to watch or one to ignore. In an environment like this, it was likely that you would become extremely single-minded, to the exclusion of anything or anyone else. Everyone was there on merit and often, rival performers would test, question and comment on each other. I think, because of my faith, I did not want to get sucked into playing that game. I did not want to mistrust everyone's motives, question everything they said, tell them how much better I was doing than they were.

When you are young, insecure and desperate to be heard, you can quickly develop advanced paranoia and a deep belief in the survival of the fittest. Now I've been at Glyndebourne for many years, I can still see that old restlessness and fear in many of the first-time performers. It is a hot-house, but the air is cooler if you determine to keep your feet on the ground. More recently, on the Glyndebourne website I was described as "Jonathan Veira, a much-loved Glyndebourne artist for over 20 years." Music to the ears of any performer!

Never give in, never give up. Churchill was right. Eventually it paid off.

CHAPTER 6

After the Flood

*There are two ways to live: you can live as
if nothing is a miracle or you can live as if
everything is a miracle.*

ALBERT EINSTEIN

Performing for royalty is one of the more interesting parts of this job, because the show always takes on a different dynamic. I have not done it as much as some, and to date I have not performed in front of the Queen of England. I have, however, notched up quite a few performances in front of Scandinavian royalty

I suppose like most of us, I had read and heard a lot about Princess Diana: the fairy-tale wedding, the glamour, the charity work and also the marital problems, the negative press and all the subsequent sadness that went with the so-called People's Princess. Whatever the case and whatever the truth about one of the most controversial members of the royal family in recent history, Diana was much loved by the people of this country, as was so clearly shown after her death. I remember sitting, numb, on the settee at home when the news of her death came through.

My encounter with Diana was at a Royal Gala Performance. I was Papageno in *The Magic Flute* by Mozart for the Covent Garden Festival. We were performing it in the Masonic Hall in Covent Garden – a daring move, as, I believe, it had not been previously open to the public. Performing at the Masonic Hall meant the opera was in the round – the 2,000 audience members surrounding the action taking place in the middle of the hall. This is in contrast to the traditional proscenium-arch theatre where the audience all face the stage. Acting in the round means that you have to be constantly aware that your back is in view to as many as can see your face. (Performing Bottom in *A Midsummer Night's Dream* the next year meant many could see my Bottom too! Sorry – childish humour!) Jamie Hayes, the director, with Jane Glover, the conductor, worked together really well to meet the challenge, to make what became an outstanding production that was enjoyable from day one. We had performed the first night, and all had gone well, and the Royal Gala Performance was on night three. The buzz went around that Princess Diana and other royals would be attending.

Now to explain what I did in this opera. As Papageno, I was the central comic character, the one who made everything happen, who talked to the audience. I was the lynchpin of the opera (if I may be modest!). The first song I sang was "The Bird Catcher's Song" where Papageno playfully describes what he does for a living. He catches birds for the wicked (boo, hiss!) Queen of the Night. This is an opera where the goodies are good and the baddies are bad.

Jamie had let me do my thing in this first song, which has three verses. The first verse I sang as the cheeky chappie, turning to all the audience at various points and singing my merry song (doesn't it sound charming!). The second verse was where things got interesting. I suggested that as the audience was so close and could be got at, I would jump down from the stage and find a lady to whom I could sing romantically while sitting on the lap of the gentleman next to her. This would require me to do a very brief reconnaissance job to identify the victim in advance.

Situations like this are a very hit-and-miss affair, but generally I have a high incidence of hits, fortunately. The first night had gone well, with a lady playing very gauche and twittery – "Oh, please, I don't want all this attention!" – but clearly loving every minute of it. The gentleman was also terribly accommodating, as the full weight of JV was thrust upon him without warning. The rest of the audience applauded wildly while thanking the Lord above that it wasn't them.

The night of the Royal Gala, I had some unexpected visitors. Because of the strangeness of the situation in the Masonic Hall, many of us shared a dressing room. So I sat with three or four others in this rather austere room, getting dressed and putting on my make-up, making final preparations about an hour before the show. Then into the room walked two rather large men, both about six foot three and heavily built. They came across to me directly. They were men of few words but very forceful ones. They said, in a slight South London brogue and with a level of menace that can only be described as, well, "menacing":

"We saw what you did the other night, going and sitting on somebody's lap, and we *strongly* suggest – and we do mean *strongly* – that you don't even think about that with HRH – or else…"

They departed hastily, whereupon the helpful colleagues in my dressing room said, in a way that only singers can: "Go on, Jon – do it!"

Well, you can imagine. All I could think about then was avoiding Princess Di. It must be made clear here that I cannot see on stage without glasses and I don't get on with contact lenses. (This is ever since one folded in my eye during *Falstaff* in 1992 in Act One, Scene One and stayed there for all seventeen and a half minutes of the scene!) So I thought: "Avoid the tiaras! You'll be safe then."

I ran on from the side for the beginning of my first aria and all I was thinking was: "I can't go near Diana, I can't go near Diana, *don't* go near Diana."

I sang the first verse. All went well. I could see a sparkling white dress on my left-hand side. I assumed that was her royal personage, so made my way to the opposite side. I sat on the lap of a gentleman and made my approaches to the lady in the ball-gown next to him. To my disquiet, I received absolutely zero response from her and indeed the audience – unlike previous performances. For a performer this is very disconcerting, but you have to remember that audiences vary and you still have to continue to do your job – whatever the response. They often show their appreciation after the show, but may not be so vocal during. On these Royal Gala occasions the audience often take their cue from the royals present.

I cut my losses and was making my way back to the stage when it suddenly occurred to me I hadn't looked at the gentleman on whose lap I had sat. I turned to look and realized that he was a familiar face. He was the man who had handed me my degree certificate at the Royal Albert Hall in 1982. It was the Duke of Kent. I had sat on the lap of the Duke of Kent! Was I completely bonkers? The performance went as performances go and the audience showed their quiet appreciation.

After this was the presentation. We were shown to a room where we would be presented to the royal party and a few words would be exchanged. I was the last in the line, so I saw Diana approaching from afar. She was truly, truly beautiful. I heard her speaking polite words to the people before me. Then suddenly, on seeing me, she pointed with what seemed to be uncharacteristic familiarity and said in a louder voice:

"You! You lunatic. If you'd sat on my lap I would have died!"

"Actually, I think *I* would have died, your Royal Highness," I replied coyly.

We then chatted for about five minutes about the music she really liked, as she wasn't a huge opera fan, but I think she had genuinely enjoyed our efforts that night. The Duke of Kent came afterwards, leaned forwards and said:

"You were the chap who sat on my lap, weren't you?"

"Yes, your Graciousness – I'm so sorry."

"Actually, I rather enjoyed it!" he replied with a wry smile, slightly the worse for wear after a long night at the opera!

I thought after this encounter that I might call my autobiography *A Lunatic, by Royal Decree*. However, I also thought of the words, *Off With His Head!*

I got home very late that night and for some reason I felt the need to write this story down. I didn't want to forget it. I didn't want to remember it wrongly and tell some kind of perverted version of it so as to make myself look better. I wanted to remember it as it happened. Maybe I had some notion of how important the experience would be for me in the future. Meeting Diana had been an extraordinary experience for me.

Language is terribly important. Some words, like "extraordinary", are so overused, misunderstood, or open to hot debate and controversy that we put them in a drawer marked "danger", or worse, we simply ignore them altogether. A word, in its simplest form, is our frail, maybe childlike, always human way of trying to explain something to someone else.

Take the word "miracle", for example. What is the first thing that comes into your head at the mention of that word? Angels, a fairy godmother, the baby Jesus, a preacher in a suit on TV, Lourdes? Like all things profound, beyond our immediate grasp, above and beyond us, we have made a good job of reducing the word "miracle" to something akin to magic, a Cinderella moment, a golden slipper – a miracle! But, a miracle could be a mother welcoming her son home from bitter fighting in Afghanistan; it could be a baby that makes it out of intensive care in spite of the doctor's professional expectations; or it could be something above or beyond what we dared to hope, pray or dream could be our reality, given the situation we find ourselves in – an outcome that leaves us with renewed hope or a lasting impression of goodness in our life.

I am careful with words, perhaps because I study them so long and hard in so many different languages for a living, perhaps because they can very easily assume a life of their own. This being said, the following are the short facts of the situation I found myself in at this point in my life. I was, without warning, taken very ill. I was in a coma. The prognosis of the doctors working with me was dire, but then I got better, much to everyone's amazement.

Here we go again – there is another of those words: "amazing"! That word now lives in the same place in our language as "awesome" and "incredible"; it is overused and lacking its original meaning or import. I have no idea why these words have come to carry so little weight and why they are used to describe every experience, from visiting the Pencil Museum in Keswick to a Domino's Pizza meal deal or a sunset in Barbados (now that *is* amazing). Perhaps we now lack the vocabulary to express what we are actually feeling.

To put the coma in context, Glyndebourne and the Friends of Covent Garden had sponsored me to go to the National Opera Studio. Very few singers here or abroad ever get to go there for specialist training. It is a highly prized, very exclusive club – a finishing school for opera singers. At the Queen Elizabeth Hall in London, in the final concert of the year, I had been reviewed in the *Guardian* as sounding very much like the great Swedish baritone Ingvar Vixell. A great compliment. From the National Opera Studio I was booked to start preparations for the *Marriage of Figaro* at Glyndebourne. Full steam ahead… apart from the iceberg.

It also seems ironic to me that I am trying to tell you about a time in my life, for much of which I was in a coma. Of course, you see the flaws in that: the patient in a hospital bed is really the stillest part of the drama as the patient is, by definition, waiting. The real perspective and action surrounds the person at the patient's bedside and the doctors and nurses who are making the decisions, doing what needs to be done. In a sense this stops being my story and becomes their story.

After the Flood

So why not let me introduce you to the person by my bedside at that time – my wife Sue? Here she is, telling the story as it affected our lives:

You remember the date when your world turns
upside down because it is an ordinary day that
suddenly twists into something quite different; a
day when you have to stop living life as it is – in
the sense of getting something for dinner, talking
to a friend on the phone, waiting outside the
school gate or nursery for your son – all of that
stuff becomes suspended, a freeze frame which
you leave behind for a world of flashing lights
and a stretcher.

It was Thursday, 22 June 1989 and Jonathan
had arrived home from a normal day rehearsing
at Glyndebourne. He had a splitting headache.
The next day was my birthday and, despite feeling
groggy, he started off by celebrating the morning
with a gift. Even so, it was clear that he was in
no shape to get to rehearsals that day, so I called
Glyndebourne. It was a gorgeous sunny day and
I was out in the garden with our son Matthew,
nearly two years old. Just after lunch I was
planning to take him to the pool with a friend, so
I went to tell Jonathan.

When I found him, it was clear that Jonathan
was really not well. He was not making any sense
(it is possible to tell!). I called our doctor to the

house and she saw Jonathan alone while I kept
Matthew busy. A few minutes later I was handed
a prescription for antibiotics (in case it was an
infection), the doctor assuring me that Jonathan
had a dose of flu. In June? She calmed my fears,
saying he should rest, so I let her out and left him
to sleep it off. By early evening my friend Judy
had arrived. I went upstairs to check on Jonathan
and to let him know that we were going to get a
takeaway for the evening. He was unconscious
and he had been sick. Trying to keep calm, I
phoned the duty doctor who told me flatly, "Just
ring the hospital, there is nothing I can do."

Oh. I dialled 999, feeling tension knot my
stomach tight. The ambulance arrived and there
then followed a kind of tense comedy of errors as
the ambulance men tried to work out how to get
Jonathan's impressive body on a stretcher down a
flight of narrow stairs with a tight turn at the top.

I wanted help, not just a kind ambulance
man used to this kind of trauma, but much more
than that. I grabbed our church contact list, Judy
holding Matthew in her arms.

"You go, I'll look after Matthew," she told me.

"Judy, I don't know where I am going or for
how long; please ask the church to pray."

Once you enter an ambulance, you are not in
your own life any more, you may as well have
handed your passport over at a checkpoint and

said, "I am in your hands now."

Blue flashing lights casting eerie shadows
on our faces, people trying to rouse Jonathan,
shining a light in his eyes, their body language
telling me all I did not want to know. This is
not right, he is not right. What is the frame of
reference for unresponsiveness like this? Is it a
brain haemorrhage?

Now there are swing doors and Jonathan
is wheeled away for more tests, me left in a
side room with some dog-eared copies of OK
magazine. Not OK at all.

I made a phone call to keep busy, to hear
someone's voice. I called our little church home
group that would meet midweek. I wanted to ask
them to be praying for Jonathan. Within an hour,
Mike, our home group leader, arrived and swept
me into a bear hug until I cried the darkness out.

Our vicar, David Bracewell, also arrived, sat
alongside, waited, prayed. Our parents would
have come straight away too, but my blurred
logic was not to tell them just yet – not until I
knew what was wrong. I did not want to worry
them. Typical me.

So there we were, Mike, his wife Ruth, our
vicar and me, watching, waiting, praying until
time felt like it had expanded into eternity. Then
a doctor came and said they were fairly sure that
Jonathan had viral encephalitis, but it might

be meningitis. They would need to do a lumbar puncture to be sure. The only light moment came when the doctor, with a serious face, intoned:

"We have done a comprehensive brain scan and we can find nothing of any significance. We will need to do further tests."

"Nothing of any significance?" I laughed. "How rude!"

I then had to explain how Jonathan would love that. It was absolutely Jonathan's sense of humour!

About 3 a.m. in the morning, another doctor told us that it was definitely viral encephalitis. He said that there was no treatment for what Jonathan had except for one drug, which might or might not have any effect on the strain of virus they were dealing with.

I was unaware that while all this was going on, the news was flying around all our friends and church family. People were praying – by themselves, or with groups of friends. One of the people praying for Jonathan was another lovely friend, Sian, a doctor. She knew the procedures that Jonathan would likely go through, particularly the lumbar puncture. Bearing in mind Jonathan's size, she knew that this would be difficult and would best be performed by someone with plenty of experience. So, she prayed specifically that the Head of A&E would perform *the procedure, as they would be likely to have that experience – which is exactly what happened. The next day, this is the conversation I heard between the admitting doctor and another junior:*

Admitting Doctor: "This guy came into A&E, he was a big man and I knew I had to do a lumbar puncture. I really did not want to do it. I was standing there with the needle in my hand and the Head of A&E taps me on the shoulder and asks if I would like to hand over. Phew!"

Junior Doctor (incredulous): "What time was that?"

Admitting Doctor: "About ten or eleven at night."

Junior Doctor (more incredulous): "What? He is never in after five in the afternoon and even if he is, you positively never see him after five on a Friday!"

Wow! That sounds really freaky if you haven't come across this kind of thing before!

Jonathan, meanwhile, was unaware of any of this. He was in a deep coma. The next day the doctor asked me what he did for a living.

"He's an opera singer," I said proudly.

The doctor shuffled his feet, looked at the ground and said flatly: "I don't think he will be any more. He is a very sick man."

This was closely followed by a good dose of British bravado from the nurse who, seeing the

*colour drain from my face, said a touch too
brightly:*

*"Oh, my dear, it may not be that bad. We got
a postcard from a man who was in the ward
with viral encephalitis last year. Do you know, he
wrote it himself!"*

Now I knew we were in a proper pickle.

*No one is immune to the kind of tragedy
that leaves a hurricane trail of permanent and
irrevocable damage through a life, or should I say
lives. Sitting in the hospital I knew this. I was
thinking of a friend of mine who lost her husband
in a train accident. She was eight months
pregnant. Ordinary days are more of a gift than
we realize until they knot up in the middle and we
would give anything just to be washing the dishes
like we did before the hurricane.*

*I was so astounded and comforted by the
stream of people who stood with me and stood
beside Jonathan's bed. I was never left alone and
neither was our son, and for that I am beyond
grateful. People travelled for miles to be near
Jonathan. His great mate Nick Whitehouse
rushed down from Leicester to sit by him as he
lay in the coma – I'm not even sure how he found
out in the first place. We only found out about his
visit some time later. Our friend Roger Sutton,
at that time the Minister of Altrincham Baptist
Church, came with his friend Ian Dunn to pray at*

Jonathan's bedside. He dropped everything, drove
for four hours, went to the hospital, popped in
to see me and then drove straight back. When he
visited me at home, he reassured me:

"He is going to be all right, Sue."

It sounded good to me, but not very likely.
How could he say so with such conviction? This
may sound a bit freaky again, but he had been
praying by Jonathan's bedside. He apparently had
got quite passionate in his praying and he had
prayed along the same lines that the people in the
Bible prayed, the ones who had personally known
Jesus; audacious prayers:

"Jonathan, in the name of Jesus, get up!"

As Roger prayed this, Jonathan had suddenly
sat bolt upright, from nowhere. Then he flopped
back down again! Roger jumped back in
amazement. Jonathan was not back, but it was
an encouraging sign, like a voice saying, "I am
listening to you."

I had not slept at all Friday night and felt a
tremendous need to be with our son Matthew,
who had already endured watching two parents
disappear in an ambulance. My dear friend, Sally,
who has known me since we were five, came to
look after us and I slept at home on the Saturday
night. First thing on the Sunday morning I rang
the ward to see how Jonathan was doing.

"He is awake," a nurse told me in a voice that

sounded as surprised as I now felt.

A doctor had been doing pin tests on
Jonathan, calling his name. He nearly fell over
when Jonathan replied groggily, "Yes?"

The doctor scrambled to get other doctors and
they all stood over his bed. Viral encephalitis is
somewhat like the brain drowning, wiping out
memories, control commands, default settings
– like someone spilling a full mug of hot coffee
all over your laptop. The doctors could not
understand why Jonathan was able to respond
at all. According to their experience, the extent of
the illness indicated that he was going to be sick
for a long while, possibly dying or likely to be left
severely brain damaged.

It transpired that Jonathan's brain had
survived this drowning intact. His brain was
still full of his life and all the opera he had so
painstakingly learned for so long. He remembered
everything apart from the time in the coma. When
I arrived at the hospital, the attending doctor was
still shaking his head, but beaming all over his
face at the same time.

The Consultant gathered the medical team
around Jonathan's bed. There was considerable
agitation from everyone as they tried to reason
away what they were seeing. Had Jonathan been
drunk? Could he have been given drugs at work
without knowing it? Could the tests have been

With Mum – in my underwear again!

Cousin Simeon, sister Ruth and a random snowman. I clearly wasn't impressed '62/'63.

A houseful as usual. Me with sister Ruth, Dad (standing), Uncle Ted, Auntie Edie and some family friends.

Me on top of a coal bunker – looking like I am about to sing an aria!

Dad and me – looks like I am sticking my tongue out at some passer by!

First "official" photograph – black hair and much promise.

Photo: Mike Thornton

Cigars and whisky… but only on stage chaps! In *Lulu* at Glyndebourne.

Photo: Mike Hoban

Playing the part of Kecal alongside the gentleman who is Sir Norman Bailey. *The Bartered Bride* Glyndebourne Festival 1999.

Photo: Mike Hoban

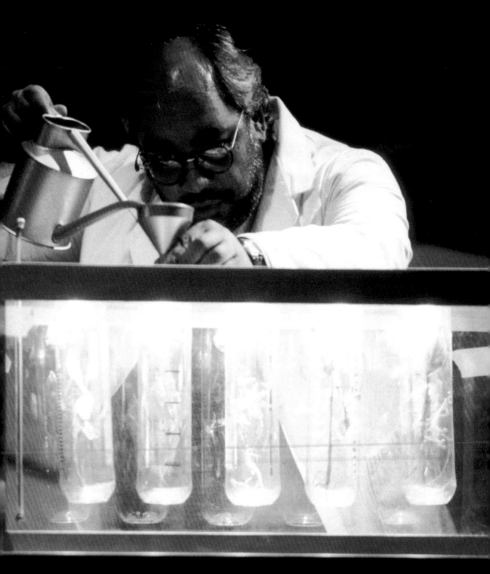

The Doctor – a dodgy genetic engineer – in *Zoe*.
Glyndebourne Opera / Channel 4.

Falstaff – Glyndebourne on Tour 2009.

Photo: Bill Cooper for Glyndebourne Productions Ltd

"Yes you sir! Row J seat 32!" Actually, Don Magnifico in *La Cenerentola* – Glyndebourne on Tour 2010.

Photo: Robbie Jack for Glyndebourne Productions Ltd

In my beloved Lake District.

My Stevie Wonder impression! Such a laugh!

Photo: Kate Kennington Steer

Sipping tea as the aged Don Pasquale – Glyndebourne on Tour 2011.
Photo: Robert Workman

In full flight in *An Audience with JV* – recounting how they "flew" me
into *L'Elisir d'Amore* in Leipzig.

wrong? They questioned me and they questioned the Consultant.

"No," insisted the Consultant. "I did those tests myself and I know without any doubt that this man had viral encephalitis and was a very sick young man."

Then, addressing Jonathan: "I am not a man of faith, but I know that you are – judging by the stream of visitors that have been to see you and pray by your bedside! Something happened here and the only word that I can find to describe it is 'miraculous'."

The young doctors did not like this word but he repeated it.

"When you cannot explain it any other way – and we can't – it is the only word you can use."

Jonathan had lost two and a half days from his life, nothing more, nothing less. The tide had receded from his brain, leaving some "debris" behind – odd bouts of irritability and uncharacteristic bad temper for the next few months. At one point I was left wondering if his personality had changed, as he failed to observe the social boundaries that were in place before he got sick. If he disagreed he just kept on… and on… and on arguing!

There were other pressures. I had just taken a two-year unpaid leave of absence from the Civil Service to be with our young son Matthew full *time, starting that month. I had three days left at work. Jonathan was a freelance opera singer and, as any freelancer knows only too well, no work equals no money. We had enough in the bank to buy groceries for about two weeks and that was that. I would have to ask for my job back.*

Except I didn't. People unobtrusively, quietly, often without us knowing who they were, started giving us money to tide us over. We didn't have to ask – they just gave. Day by day we received the money that covered our mortgage and daily life, just enough to last us until Jonathan returned to work, like the Lord's Prayer: "Give us this day our daily bread."

Our daily bread showed up through the generosity of others. We were moved and so encouraged. We experienced God's love through people time and time again. For example, Sian, the doctor who had prayed for Jonathan's successful lumbar puncture, sent us a cheque for a very specific, seemingly random amount of money: £272. She wrote on the envelope, "For mortgage and related expenses". She felt that God wanted her to send the money for precisely that purpose. When I totalled our mortgage and endowment policies they added up to £271.27. I was amazed. The cheque that our friend gave us almost exactly covered our mortgage expenses, that I didn't exactly know myself! I joked to

Jonathan, "God overshot our mortgage by 73 pence."

When I told Sian, she explained. As she had been praying for Jonathan to get better, she had a very strong sense that she should write a cheque to help us. The amount that was buzzing in her head was £272. Before she wrote the cheque, our friend had one of those arguments with God:

"Why £272? Why not £275 or £270? It is so odd!"

God definitely has a sense of humour, or maybe he just likes non-round numbers. Whatever his reason, we were left open-mouthed at God meeting our needs through the kindness and generosity of people. Jonathan is a very unassuming person. He would never think that he meant enough to people that they would go out of their way for him. He just did not think of himself like that. When people dropped what they were doing to be with him, or children sent him letters, drawings and sweets to make him feel better, he was deeply touched. Healed in other ways by that and moved by the kindness of so many.

As I said, though, hurricanes leave trails. Jonathan had recovered, life in his head intact, but life as he knew it was much altered by his illness. He had disappeared from the opera scene for about six months and in his absence, the scenery had changed.

Being a creative business full of people who imagine fantastic things for a living, I had some understanding of how the rumour mill had been working overtime. The full extent became clear to us when Jonathan turned up for a rehearsal to be met with the comment:

"Oh! I was told you had died of Mad Cow disease after eating a contaminated burger at McDonalds."

Nice one. In the time it had taken Jonathan to fall ill and recover, he had gone from being "the most promising singer" to a doubtful "Well, we may be able to use you as second spear carrier in Act Two."

Jonathan had lost his agent too, so there was no one looking for work for him and the prospect of meaningful work seemed remote. By now, I was pregnant with our second child, Dan, and we were having the inevitable conversations about my return to the workplace.

The thing about Jonathan is that he does not give up and whatever the job, he always shows up. I think that is a lesson in itself. Rather than throw his toys out of the pram and walk away, Jonathan duly showed up for rehearsals at the Buxton Festival. He was to appear in the chorus of The Italian Girl in Algiers by Rossini and understudy the main role of Mustafa (now one of *his keynote roles), as well as play a small part in Handel's* Aggripina.

This was a really demoralizing period of time for Jonathan. Accepting this difficult step backwards, dealing with the daily comments and the fact that his contemporaries were miles ahead of him was hard. However, as a direct result of Jonathan's showing up and working hard, Jane Glover, the conductor of The Italian Girl in Algiers, *went out of her way to help him back on track over the next year or so.*

What would we do without those who, noticing that our journey has become hard, choose to walk the extra mile alongside, come hell or high water?

Hi, JV back again. I was gone for a while, things got a little hazy and when I woke up everyone's jaw was on the floor and they had all grown much, much taller. Or at least my retina was telling me that I was now Jack among giants.

I woke up to find myself in my underpants (those underpants again…) in a bed surrounded by doctors who were talking about me in hushed voices. My cousin Simeon was sitting next to me, having slept overnight in his car. He was best man at my wedding. We are very close, more like brothers than cousins, and I knew that he would understand when I told him that I had to get back to work. I struggled to sit up and get out of bed, but he kept crying, saying, "We nearly lost you! You have to get some rest."

I was meant to be in an opera. Now I had woken up in a disaster movie or one of those episodes of *Casualty* where you can guarantee to find someone looking wan in a hospital bed. Sue turned up and she was crying; everyone was crying. I was no longer destined to be a vegetable. Sue assured me that her tears had nothing to do with the life insurance that she had been looking forward to claiming!

Apart from the fact that everyone had grown to gigantic proportions while I was out of commission, it was clear that my life, our lives, had changed. The question was, by how much?

For many weeks afterwards, apparently, I was short-tempered and downright nasty with some family and friends. In particular, I was terribly rude to Nick (now Bishop of Bradford) and Linda Baines. Sorry, chaps. My sister remembers me not being able to read the paper – the words just didn't make any sense and she was concerned that I wouldn't be able to read scripts again, or learn music. I don't actually remember all these details; it must have been part of the brain-healing process and maybe the frustrations of my recovery causing some of my bad temper.

So, why me? What was so special about me? Was this a "healing" or did I get better because I am a strong person? What is the factual evidence apart from hearsay and words used in the heat of the moment?

Was it just wishful thinking?

The facts are as Sue recorded them at the time. She noted them down in a scientific way because that is her background. She is not given to flights of fancy nor religious mania. I am neither special nor strong enough to wish myself better. In fact I was out cold in a coma!

I can't tell you why I was the only one on that ward to be healed. I can't tell you why my own sister hasn't had a debilitating illness removed from her – despite similar amounts of prayer.

I suppose my response is that of the blind man in the Bible. After Jesus healed him, he was faced with so many questions. What? When? Where? How? Who? Why? He replied simply: "Once I was blind, but now I can see."

What more can I say definitively about that life-changing time in 1989? I'm here, over twenty years later. I have two more fantastic sons and I am still married to Sue – that wonderful long-suffering woman who stood by my bed.

I am deeply, deeply grateful to God for the extra time I have been given.

To move on, six months later the BBC's *Songs of Praise* was visiting our town and researching local stories of faith and interest. Our vicar, David Bracewell, suggested me and the story of my recovery, among others, and the Beeb picked it up. They came and interviewed Sue and me at our home with Matt. He was just two at the time, running around excitedly, making sure he was the centre of attention for the cameras, and sure enough, he was. It was on this programme in 1989 that I first sang the famous hymn "How Great Thou Art", which began a relationship with *Songs of Praise* that has lasted for more than twenty years. I have visited Israel, Austria and many locations all over Britain with them and it has been great fun.

In so many ways this was a life-changing experience, not just for me but for all those around me – immediate family, friends, and well beyond. It changed the focus of my life, very much like a camera changing its focus from portrait to landscape, from zoom to wide angle. The same elements are in the image, but the focus has changed. It enabled me to begin to see what was really important, who was really important and how I wanted to spend the rest of my life. The coma came upon me in minutes, but the effects would last a lifetime and it changed my life completely. How long do we have? We really don't know, but I became determined to attempt to live a life for today and be gracious and honest with the people I came into contact with. I know I fail at that and many other things, all too often, but with God's grace I will keep trying. That's the thing about God's grace – it doesn't give up.

We will never forget the people who made such a great difference to our lives during this period: we received so much, from the sweet sent by a small child ("to make Jonathan feel better"), to the many generous cash gifts and cherished words of encouragement. One dear friend did our shopping for us and bought some freezer meals – at the same time as doing her own first shop with newborn twins! Just one example of how so many friends and family did what they could, in such practical ways, to help us through this difficult time. Sue's brother Nigel was visiting from Hong Kong around this time and was very concerned about the money that people were giving us.

"How will they pay it all back, Mum?" was his perplexed question.

My dear mother-in-law got it just right when she said: "They won't have to, son. It's what these people do."

By this she meant Christians, and she was so right. We have learned from the extraordinary generosity of others how to be generous. Such generosity had enabled us to buy our house in 1987 and, as a result, we try to show similar kindness to others.

It would be fair to say that post illness, I am a very different person to the young man who was so focused on obtaining success and getting to the top of the tree in the operatic world.

From a career point of view, Glyndebourne were absolutely brilliant. They paid me some money when they had no obligation to do so. They waited and then, after a period of time, welcomed me back. So especially to Sir George and Lady Mary Christie – a huge and heartfelt thank you.

Three things I have learned from this experience:

You can be surprised by how much people care and

how kind they can be.

You never know what tomorrow is going to bring.

Make the most of the time that you have, today.

CHAPTER 7

Crossing the Language Barrier

Massenet feels it as a Frenchman, with powder and minuets. I shall feel it as an Italian, with desperate passion.

PUCCINI

(QUOTED IN M. CARNER, *PUCCINI*, 1974)

Life as an opera singer is always mysterious. Or, should I say, when you are an opera singer life can be very odd. I am reasonably sure that you have never been asked to tell a joke, standing in front of an audience of 2,000 people, wrapped only in a towel with shaving cream on your head, while the stage crew manage a complicated scenery change behind you. No? I didn't think so. I was playing Don Magnifico, Cinderella's wicked stepfather in a great production by Irina Brooks, daughter of the famous director Peter Brooks. During rehearsals, when everything seems like a good idea, Irina had asked:

"Jonathan, can you do a bit of Vaudeville?"

139

An innocent question and one to which I rather hastily said, "Yes."

"Well, we have to bring in a curtain between two of the acts. It's going to take a bit of time. Do you think you could keep the audience engaged, maybe tell them a joke or two? In character, of course?"

At the end of the preceding act, I was to perform a duet with the baritone while we were in a sauna with towels wrapped around us. It seemed perfectly natural, then, to walk out in front of the audience at the Swedish National Opera dressed just in that towel with a dollop of shaving cream, like a Mr Whippy, on top of my head. And perfectly natural to tell them a joke about a sixty-five-year-old man called Fred who goes to the doctor:

"Doctor, I just want to check that everything is in working order. I'm getting on a bit now, you know."

The doctor checks the man over, hmming and harring, prodding and poking away. "You seem absolutely fine, Fred – right as rain. But tell me this, my good fellow: are you at one with God, and are you at one with yourself?"

"Oh, I certainly am at one with God," says Fred. "In fact, we are very close. In the middle of the night, when I have to do a wee, I go to the loo and – *poof!* – the light comes on, and – *poof!* – the light goes right off again, all of its own accord."

"Amazing," says the doctor. "That is quite incredible."

The doctor is so intrigued that he decides to call

Fred's wife, Janet. "Janet," he says, "I've just had Fred in. He says that he and God are on such good terms that when he goes for a wee in the middle of the night, the light comes on and goes off again for him, all of its own accord. Don't you find that incredible?"

Janet groans, "Oh no! He's been weeing in the fridge again."

It had worked – an Englishman telling a joke in English in the middle of an Italian opera to Swedes in Sweden! They laughed long and loud – no doubt bemused by the whole spectacle. After that I spoke to them in Danish. The best way to make a Swedish audience laugh is to do an impression of the Danish language. The Swedish think that Danish is not so much a language as a throat disease. The Danish tell exactly the same joke about the Swedes – really! And let's not talk about the Norwegians. They all speak roughly (I do mean roughly) the same language, but don't like to admit it. I know that I will get into trouble with my Scandinavian friends, but there you go.

Anyway, I did my ten minutes, the scene was changed, I got a big pat on the back and the reviews loved the "English comedian". They didn't really comment on the singing.

Why is it that in the movies today, the baddie is often English, the romantic one is often French and the passionate one is often Italian or South American? Languages say it all, literally. Over the past twenty-six years I have had to say it all in up to eight languages: Italian, French, Spanish, Czech, German, Russian, Swedish, and let's not forget, English.

Now imagine you do not just have to adopt an accent and make your character credible, but actually "speak" the language so that a native believes you are one of his countrymen, not just a graduate from the academy of silly talks! My son Dan has a friend who went into his French GCSE oral exam and when asked a question in French, responded in English, but with a French accent (think *Allo, Allo*). Needless to say, he failed, as would I. Singing a whole opera amounts to an awful lot of words to translate word for word so that you understand every word you sing and, therefore, grasp the intention of the sentence so that you can act out what is being said.

Unlike a Hollywood movie that may be overdubbed for the Chinese market, or a French film noir that is given English subtitles, operas are nearly always performed in the language in which they were written, apart from companies like the English National Opera, who perform all of their operas in English. In the same way as a group of international business-people will err towards a language common to all of them, opera companies can be confident of employing performers for their next production from as far afield as Brazil and Japan, sure in the knowledge that everyone has learned the same score and is singing the same language. Think how much time and drama you are saving, plus the original intent of the libretto is preserved along with the rhythm of the language.

Sometimes, when I am involved in a live performance, the opera is being recorded for a knowledgeable radio or TV audience, so there is very little room for error. Singing in a foreign language is a bit like walking a tightrope over Niagara Falls: it's better when you don't look down. It must be made absolutely clear that I don't – I really don't – speak all of these languages. Strangely, I am most definitely *not* a talented linguist, but I do seem to have a very good ear for languages. I get by in Italian, French and German, but the rest? I work very hard. However, I do seem to have the knack to fool most of the people most of the time, and I put that down to my aforementioned skill at mimicry! In Lyon, I performed, in Czech, a trilogy of operas by Janáček. A guy came up after the first night and spoke to me in Czech.

"No, no, no – I don't speak Czech," I replied hastily in French.

"Oh!" he said, "I thought you were from a town south of Prague."

As the tightrope performer feels his way along a rope section by section, I learn my parts by feeling out the sounds, the phonics, over and over again until I know a section and am ready to move on to the next. It is painstaking work, taking hours and hours and months and months, involving many late nights and early mornings. My aim is that the language comes naturally and is not a barrier to my being able to assume the role with confidence.

I am learning *Don Pasquale* as I write. Much of the Italian language is familiar to me now after so many years of specializing in the Italian repertoire. I can hear the rhythm of the words, key phrases and intonation. So you learn your lines in the age-old way, poring over the words until they become second nature. This, of course, while your family goes mad with you singing, playing and humming the score for *months* before you start rehearsals. Then you take your interpretation to your first rehearsal where you are introduced either to your nemesis or your salvation – the language coach!

If you are rehearsing an Italian opera, say *L'elisir d'amore* by Donizetti, you will be working with a language coach who knows the language a lot better than you do. But, the reality is that a language coach who grew up in the north of Italy will pronounce certain words differently to a coach who learned Italian in a school in Rome. There is obviously a variation of dialect between north and south, with a difference of emphasis. One says vowels should always be open and the other says vowels should always be closed. The term "always" is what is so interesting, as with language there is constant change. Of course there are constants, but these become arguable, and arguments certainly occur from time to time about pronunciation!

British people will instantly understand this. Do you pronounce the word for a tub of hot water to be enjoyed before bedtime with a long vowel – b*aa*th – or a short vowel – b*a*th? In opera, when the rehearsals begin, so does the debate. During one of my early years at Glyndebourne when I was understudying *Falstaff*, I had a wonderful Italian coach called Rosetta. I had learned a smattering of Italian at college, enough to query her as we came to our first *"zz"* word. The simple rule is that on most occasions, though there are exceptions, *"zz"*s in Italian are pronounced as a *"tz"*, so in this case I was pronouncing *pozzo* (which means "well") as *"poTzo"*.

"No, no, Jon-a-tan," quibbled Rosetta, "de word ees *poDzo*, not dat horreeble *poTzo*."

"OK, Rosetta, originally I was told it should be *poTzo*," I replied, mentally making a note to change the language entry in my head, until one of my colleagues piped up timidly:

"Er, well, actually here in my English–Italian dictionary it says that it's *poTzo*."

"No, no, no!" implored Rosetta, closing the dictionary with Italian style and confidence. "We would never say eet like dat!"

And so the dance continues. Learning an opera with a language coach plus a conductor and a music director is a bit like being on a peace mission between Palestine and Israel. A copious amount of diplomacy is required. I would be learning a German part from *Die Entführung aus dem Serail* by Mozart and the German librettist Christoph Friedrich Bretzner, while my German language coach would stop me over and over again:

"No, zis is wrong. Again, please!"

Then all of a sudden the clouds would break, the

sun would come out and she would say:

"Got it! Got it!"

I had absolutely no idea what I had changed to make her day, but I had obviously stopped insulting her country and its history and language! I still remember the words twenty years later, so she must have done something right.

If the opera were in French, there would be a significant increase in the amount of opinions as to the right way to say anything. If there were ten people in the room there would be eleven opinions! What is agreed is that the singer is always being told the better way to do or say something. You learn your part with all diligence one way, go to another opera house and you are implored to do it differently. That's just the way it is and eventually it gives you even more ways of understanding it and performing the piece.

As you become more established you learn which battles to fight and when to give in. Eventually, you have to make each role your own. You listen, consult, adapt, but ultimately you have to take responsibility for your interpretation of the character. You cannot simply fall back on the line, "The director made me do it this way." (Though sometimes one doesn't have a choice; it is ultimately the director's and conductor's show and you are there to fulfil their vision of the piece.)

The next challenge involves "recitativo". This is a trick that composers and librettists use to swiftly advance the plot in an opera. It is speech often accompanied by harpsichord and cello, sometimes with orchestra. Recitativo is basically used to tell the story of a piece. It's the narrative that is the link between the aria, the duet, the trio or the ensemble. The aria is usually one idea often repeated over and over for emphasis.

A character's delivery of recitativo should be conversational and, as such, must possess a natural cadence – the rhythmic sequence or flow of sounds in language. The words of languages like Italian and Czech dance to their own tune. It is up to the singer to listen and learn how to dance in time. Like the dancer rehearsing steps until the dance becomes as natural as breathing, so the singer engages with the words of recitativo until they are his words.

If you are learning a language, it is best to listen to the way native people speak it. Do they head for the verb or the noun in a sentence? If the verb is "to walk", do they emphasize the verb itself or do they give the person walking the priority – "*I'm* going to walk"?

If you think about English, the emphasis that we put on an individual word or words completely changes the meaning of a sentence.

"I'm going to *walk*" implies that we will not be running or taking a cab.

"I *am* going to walk" might be a statement of belief from someone who has had a car accident and who, before long, will be free of their wheelchair.

"*I'm going to walk!*" might be a deliberate statement conveyed to an elderly relative who is hard of hearing.

Depending on the production and direction of an opera, you may be required to deliver your lines in a stylized or more contemporary fashion. Think of the difference between performing *The Merchant of Venice* within the confines of sixteenth-century Italy or updated to the location of London's Stock Market in the 1990s. Opera is not real life, but it must imitate whatever life it is presenting.

As anyone who has translated an ancient classic text, from the Bible to Shakespeare, will tell you, there is a fine balance between maintaining the credibility of the piece as it was intended to be and updating it for a contemporary audience. In my opinion, a new concept for the production of a classic opera should fall humbly in line behind the text and the music, or at the very least favour the original meaning, rather than seeking to replace it with something newer and better.

Initially, when I approach a new part or production, all I am asking is: What is this story about? How can I tell this story as it was intended to be told? The best moments in opera come when everyone is working towards this end. David McVicar's production of *Figaro* in which I played the part of Dr Bartolo for Covent Garden comes instantly to mind. It was an exceptionally moving production where the text, the music, the concept, the staging all came together in an unusually profound way. His mantra was always, "What is the story? Tell me the story."

Equally, a new concept for a very familiar opera

can help you to develop as a performer. It can help an audience see diverse, previously unexplored elements of a character, a scene or a situation. One of my favourite TV series of all time was *The West Wing* written by the brilliant Aaron Sorkin. The series, starring Martin Sheen as President Bartlett, covered the staple TV subject of political drama in a whole new way. It so endeared Sheen to the nation that there was a generous groundswell of opinion that he should actually run for President! One of Bartlett's favourite phrases after dealing with a crisis such as a hurricane or the threat of war was, "OK, what's next?"

It is good to be looking ahead, thinking of different ways to do things. However, when you are producing from an original, it is best to reflect on the reasons why the original has endured. Operas like *La Bohème* and *Madame Butterfly* have so much beauty contained in universal themes that they will always move people. You do not always need to gild the lily just for the sake of it.

At best, when you rehearse something over and over again, it can become as natural as your DNA. This is especially true when you are working with a director and conductor who intrinsically know the standard you can attain and will accept nothing less. The best productions are a successful marriage of everyone pushing hard to create sublime reality.

The audience instinctively knows when you make it to the summit of sublime reality. It happened during the Glyndebourne Tour in a revival of the 1995 Peter Hall production of Rossini's *La Cenerentola* (or *Cinderella*). The original version had quickly won the love of the critics: "a performance that meets the Glyndebourne gold standard: understated, sensitive and thus deeply pleasurable" (*Daily Telegraph*).

In our 2010 Autumn Tour revival we had a lot to live up to. I was playing Cinderella's "monstrous" stepfather Don Magnifico – a miserable guy, horrible, disgusting, an essential counterpoint to the beauty and grace of Cinderella. The conductor, Enrique Mazzola, and the revival director, Lynne Hockney, knew the text and the music inside out. When that happens there are no roadblocks, no times when everyone feels slightly lost. In addition, they were never satisfied, to the point where your body and your head were crying out in a mewing kind of melodramatic unison: "What more do you want from me?"

Then the first night came and I was just blown away by how good this production was. It was worth every bit of the effort it had taken to do justice to the original.

But despite and even with all that preparation, sometimes things just go dreadfully wrong – especially when you are transitioning from one opera to another.

A classic example of "transition" came when I was finishing up our run at Glyndebourne in *Don Giovanni* and preparing for *Cosi Fan Tutte* with the Royal Opera in wonderful, wonderful Copenhagen. During one of our final performances of *Don Giovanni*, right bang in the middle of a complicated recitativo, my mind managed to link a familiar word from *Don Giovanni* to *Cosi Fan Tutte*. To my abject horror, what came out of my mouth next was more *Cosi* than *Don*.

Hearing the misplaced script, the harpsichord player accompanying me gazed across, mildly horrified as I attempted a spectacular back-flip in my mind from page 26 of *Cosi* to page 351 of *Don*. One word, a familiar word in a different context acting like a train turntable, until you realize that you should be near Lewes, East Sussex rather than on the Copenhagen waterfront!

Another time, while actually in Copenhagen, I was singing in *La Cenerentola* (*Cinderella* again), being broadcast on Danish radio, live, and suddenly there were no more words. My mind hit a comprehensive blank during a very fast text moment known as "patter", where there should be a huge amount of words in a very small amount of time. Of course, you cannot pause or hit the fast-forward button, so there you are, stuck in that moment. I drew myself up and gabbled my way through the blankness until the words came back. Happily, the Italian conductor, Maestro Carlo Andretta, was able to compensate for my momentary lapse and afterwards he clapped me on the back with a chuckle:

"Jon-a-tan, whad were you singing? I did not understand your words."

I said, "Strange, that. I didn't understand them either!"

Sometimes the mind has a mind of its own!

They say that minor car accidents happen when

151

people start to relax. The defences naturally start to lower as you near the warm hearth of home. It is logical, really: when you are happy, you tend to relax and as you relax, lapses of concentration can occur. A lapse of concentration in a complicated piece of opera, however, is no laughing matter.

> *Tutto nel mondo è burla ...*
> *Tutti gabbati!*
> *(All the world's a joke,*
> *man is born a joker,*
> *and he who laughs last, laughs longest.)*

FALSTAFF BY GIUSEPPE VERDI (ADAPTED BY ARRIGO BOITO, 1893)

The finale of *Falstaff* ends with a complicated fugue. This simply means that I start with the main theme, which is repeated by all the cast members in turn. They copy what I sing.

I was participating in a beautiful, excellent production of *Falstaff* by John Cox. There is a sense of wonder when a production is going well. When you are playing Falstaff, wonderfully jolly in your fat suit that makes you three times your normal size, there is a huge sense of relief towards the end when you are about to start this fugue. You have lost pounds in sweat just standing there. You have nearly made it.

When John Geilgud was asked about his thoughts on being a great actor, he would often reply: "I have been extraordinarily lucky." He explained that when he was on stage he would be thinking that one night the audience was going to find him out, but he vowed it would not be that night.

As *Falstaff* drew to a close, I felt just like that: "I have almost made it! They will not find me out tonight." That's what I have felt every single night I have performed. It seems to keep me going, performance after performance; it really isn't false humility. I suppose we are back to the tightrope walker who is doing just fine up on that wire until he looks down. I have not been winging it for twenty-six years, but when I am called a "firm Glyndebourne favourite", I am overcome with the wonder of it all. No one has called me a fake or a phony and told me to leave the stage. Some people are actually super-confident about what they do. I am not one of them.

Back to our Falstaff fugue. I was on the tightrope, I looked down and then I wobbled. I had wanted to do Falstaff internationally for a long time and this production in Copenhagen was like a gift to me. I so enjoyed the collaboration with musical director Michael Schønwandt, an excellent musician who truly loved Falstaff as much as I did. I had an enormous amount invested in the whole experience.

I strode forward and, as the orchestra played the glorious introduction, my mind went blank. No words. No memory of what came next. Not a single blessed word came to mind. I had to start singing, however, or no one else could sing, so I did what anyone seeking relief would do in a situation like that: I made the words up.

What it should have been was: "*Tutto nel mondo e burla.*"

What came out was: "Nelly schmar del te gango."

The singer who was due to repeat my very famous, now abridged words, looked at me with wide eyes, filled with disbelief and horror. She must have thought:

"Help! Do I sing what he sang, or do I sing what I should be singing?"

After all, she was meant to be copying me. At that point there should be merriment on the stage, and by then no one was acting. All the cast was laughing, singing. We made it through, mostly unscathed.

Let no one believe this is all that unusual. I was playing the part of Dr Kolenatý, a lawyer in *The Makropulos Affair* by Leoš Janáček, sung in Czech. It was a great opportunity to work with the distinguished Swedish soprano, Anja Silja. However, we had only one week to rehearse the entire piece. In the first act, my lawyer Kolenatý has to review a complicated court case with Silja's character, who is desperate to know her legal position in the matter at hand.

On the first night of *The Makropulos Affair*, the wonderful Andrew Davies was conducting the London Philharmonic Orchestra. Our opera was in full swing and the orchestral ostinato (a repeated and persistent phrase) was approaching fast around the bend, super speed. My phrase, which was Czech legalese, and which went on over the orchestral ostinato, was about to begin. Anja Silja looked intently at me and I thought, "What is my phrase?" I couldn't find the phrase in my head, and when this happens, eight seconds on stage feels like five hours. I looked at Andrew Davies and he threw his hands up in the air as if to say, "Sorry, Jonathan, I can't help you. Just get on with it."

I went back to the coat-hangers I have in my head, the handy pegs that I hang my words and phrases on. I was looking for a sign – where was that phrase? My dog could have prompted me if she had been there. I had sung that opera so much around the house, I am sure she knew it by heart. Round and round the house, in the shower, up and down the stairs. Then I found it. I had my phrase and all was well – after eight seconds of agony!

The production of *The Makropulos Affair* was so successful that we got an invitation to perform it in Lyon, and then I performed it again in a concert performance for Dutch radio at the Concertgebouw with the Netherlands Radio Philharmonic Orchestra. It had the "wow" factor, but that "wow" factor always represents months and months, hundreds of hours, of work. I reckon, on an hourly basis, I must be paid about £1.16 an hour.

Although I have never been diagnosed, I think I have a mild form of dyslexia, so words and notes don't come that easily to me. I cannot sight read quickly, I have to read bar by bar, not one bar ahead. I also have a slight stutter, although not when I am singing. My antidote to all of this is unadulterated hard work.

I mentioned at the beginning of this chapter that I am currently learning Don Pasquale. In twenty-six years I have never done this opera, so I am putting a huge amount of time into learning it. Last night I was up until 1.30 a.m. working on it, and then I got up at 6.00 and was back at it. That's how I do it, at first just looking at the score, searching for clues, the shape of the harmonies, the way the music twists and turns. It remains a demanding exercise – slightly easier now that I know what I am doing. It has taken time but it has been worth it. In a way it has been my own personal boot camp for nigh on thirty years, training, rehearsing, performing.

My youngest son Nick, then aged ten or so, was watching one of these talent shows where the entrants were being sent on a two-week boot camp. Turning to me, he said, "Daddy, have you had to do anything as difficult as this?"

Like Homer in *The Simpsons*, I nearly grabbed him around the neck, screaming, "Why, you little...!"

CHAPTER 8

Getting There

Travel makes a wise man better, but a fool worse.

PROVERB

I f you are filming for TV – music, soap opera, documentary, any kind of filming, really – you could be forgiven for thinking that you are making a wildlife documentary. From the moment you book your ticket, assemble your cameras and sound equipment, check in at the airport and attempt to negotiate customs, anything that can go wrong, will go wrong.

On one trip to Jerusalem we were filming a BBC *Songs of Praise* special, wanting to capture something of the history and spirit of the Holy City, something above the ordinary. This would be covered over two programmes and spawn a CD as well (*BBC Songs from the Holy Land*). On one occasion we were filming on some of the ruined walls of the city, and appropriately singing the famous song, "The Holy City". Above the sound of the backing track and the camera crane I suddenly became aware of two men running towards me. As they came closer I could see they were two orthodox Jewish men who, I later learned, were outraged that we were filming on their holy site. The fact that we had permission was simply not relevant to them. We eventually continued and I remember thinking what an extraordinary melting-pot Jerusalem is. So many different groups all laying claim to various parts of Jerusalem – as it has been for centuries.

A more light-hearted incident (but serious for me) occurred at the Paternoster Church, where you can find the Lord's Prayer uniquely written on the walls in countless languages. I was to stroll effortlessly through the corridors of this fascinating church while singing the Lord's Prayer – again to playback. Suddenly I was aware of a slight griping feeling down below. This is the fear of all performers on stage, in recording sessions and, more worryingly, on location on the top of a hill in Israel. All I could think was, "Where is the nearest loo and have I brought my Imodium?"

Suffice to say, it focuses the mind somewhat and I was terribly good on the first take. No mistakes. As the song finishes you can see the slightly worried look on my face! If the camera had followed me after the final note of the last "Amen", it would have seen me running as fast as my little legs could carry me to the nearest loo, which an assistant had located for me. Needless to say, the crew loved that.

Even when leaving Israel, I wasn't free from mishap. I was delayed for hours at customs because I had innocently told them I had a bag that came from

Scotland, and none of the officials knew where that was! The same officials then quizzed me on why I was an opera singer. That question genuinely perplexed me and became an existential one. Indeed, why *was* I an opera singer? I became deeply ironic and this did not make them happy. It was, I now realize, the wrong move. I did it to get a laugh, but there were not many laughs to be had. I was there for nearly three hours and barely caught my plane, vowing not to return in too much of a hurry.

Any time you are filming, home or abroad, you are at the mercy of trains and planes, the locals, your health, the weather, and finding out things about the area you are trying to film in that you could never have known before you left. All sorts of happy chaos ensues. Then, every so often, something extraordinary happens. Like, for instance, the time when we were filming in Jericho and a single shepherd led his sheep out across the mountain, just at sunrise, while I was standing there singing "How Great Thou Art". The hymn went on to be voted the UK's favourite by *Songs of Praise* viewers. Despite all the vagaries of filming, in that moment something special happened. What an extraordinary, challenging, beautiful and deeply disturbing place Israel is. I hope I find my way back sometime.

Another time I was at the Royal Albert Hall for a *Songs of Praise* special that was being filmed live with the BBC Concert Orchestra. Waiting backstage were Cliff Richard, Gloria Gaynor and myself. It doesn't matter how many times you have sung to an audience or been filmed, when a TV programme is going out live, the bank of nerves that you are holding in check increases. Especially when the producer of the programme gives you a pep talk just before you are due to go on:

"Big audience for this one, Jonathan. It's going out around the world and we are making a live CD from it. Don't screw it up, will you? No pressure."

Perfect. All I remember after that is walking on stage in my big jacket and my "should have gone to Specsavers" glasses, as one of my sons calls them. My mind went blank and I recall thinking: "I have no idea what I am meant to be singing!" If you watch it, you can see me open my mouth as if to say, "Oh, Lord..."

Then comes the next line: "... my God, when I in awesome wonder..."

Awesome wonder, indeed! I did another *Songs of Praise* live special from a beautiful stately home – one of those gorgeous places like Castle Howard in *Brideshead Revisited*, an elegant pile in the North of England. We were well rehearsed and it was all going swimmingly well until suddenly the lights went out. Not just one light – all the lights. Because the show was going out live, I couldn't just stop singing, so I carried on blithely making my way through "You Are The One Who Makes Me Happy" in the dark for what seemed like forever, until a BBC technician worked out how to get the lights back on. Sorry about that, viewers; slight technical hitch caused by ancient spliced wiring.

I love working with my kids... now! When they were

little, however, they would be predictably unpredictable. I have already mentioned Matt, aged two, showing off on the first *Songs of Praise*. My kids were used to our regular sessions of singing around the piano together as a family, so having a benevolent-father moment, I thought it would be a lovely idea to have them around me at the piano while we were filming a piece for *Songs of Praise at Christmas*. I was singing "When a Child is Born" (finally recorded on my Christmas CD, *O Holy Night*). Matt was fine about it, Dan a little more apprehensive, and Nick? Nick was about four or five at the time. There were no mishaps until, in the final shot, you can see little Nick tilt further and further to the right, waving at one of the cameras placed out of shot. He is waving and doing the classic "Hey look, there's a camera. I must be on TV!" Nobody yelled "Cut!"

As I was telling this story I just recalled that on the same recording session, about an hour before Nick's little performance on network TV, the electricity failed. There was a huge audience sitting around in the depths of winter. No light. No sound. No heat. All I had was a piano and Raul D'Olivera on flugel horn. So we did what any self-respecting musicians would do – we entertained the audience as best we could.

There is always something. The villagers of Oberammergau in Bavaria made a solemn promise to God that if their village survived the terrible plague epidemic that was, by then, decimating Europe, they would perform a passion play every ten years, to remember what he had done. The village was spared and they have made good on their promise ever since. The Oberammergau Passion Play is a massive undertaking in which only villagers are allowed to take part. Each production involves well over 1,000 residents, singers, musicians, carpenters and dressmakers. It is an incredible achievement and has so captured people's imaginations that tickets are snapped up years ahead.

I was very grateful then, when I found out that the BBC wanted me to go and make a film in and around the event. Now, what could possibly go wrong? When I was not filming, I spent much of my time watching what was going on, really moved by parts of it. Somehow it felt very realistic, seeing Jesus caught up in the frenzy of an angry mob.

I was staying in a hotel right out of *The Sound of Music*, near to which a local wood-carver had placed a beautiful cross. We decided to film me singing "When I Survey The Wondrous Cross" there. The director had an idea for a piece of filming where I would walk slowly through the swaying Bavarian grass up to the cross and then sing the second verse. Filming is expensive, so we got right onto it. So there I was, walking slowly through the gently swaying grass towards the cross, until someone shouted:

"Hey Jonathan! Look down. Your trousers, your trousers!"

If you are out walking in the early morning on a *Sound of Music* hill in Bavaria, you may want to note

162

that there is a profusion of dew on the grass. If you are being filmed wearing light-coloured trousers, then it's very likely you will end up looking like you have wet yourself. As I said, filming is expensive, so you have to work with what you have, where you are. There's little margin for reshoots. In the final piece, then, you first see all of me at a very "safe" distance, followed by a close-up of just my top half!

After I dried out and was safely back in the UK, a producer for CBBC approached me. They were putting together an episode of *The Tweenies* to help introduce children to opera and, he wondered, could I help at all? I had lots of ideas and before long we went on to complete a wonderful, fun programme. It featured the amazingly obliging soprano, Diana Gilchrist, and myself singing a piece from *The Magic Flute*, "Pap-pap-pap-papagena".

I am dressed as a chicken. Yes, a chicken! Years later, I still gets calls from friends whose children have been watching children's TV:

"Hey, Jonathan! I've just seen you on *The Tweenies* dressed as a chicken."

Yes. Thank you.

People who travel for work will tell you that even if you think you have all your bases covered – you have done your local research, you have planned your route, you have booked your room – staying away from home can still be a very hit-and-miss affair. In the days before the wonder of Google maps and internet bookings, the challenges were even greater. In the early days, a group of aspiring opera singers, including myself, were involved in a low-budget, nationwide Opera Eighty production of *Carmen*. I had secured the part of Morales and was also singing in the chorus. We were travelling singers taking opera to places like the Leisure Centre in Seaton, a small town in the North-East.

As we were being paid very little, we were doing it all on the cheap, sharing cars, booking B&Bs and hotel rooms together to keep costs down. All the rooms had been booked ahead to save us turning up somewhere and finding that there was no room at the inn. After a long journey down the motorway, we arrived, mid-afternoon, at the place where we had booked to stay in Seaton. It was an old English pub, only not the quaint, cosy, ancient, oak-beamed type, but rather the run-down, boarded-up version. We were in the middle of nowhere, so we had no choice but to at least knock and find out where we were booked into, hoping that maybe we had missed an inviting pub of the same name a few minutes down the road.

We knocked and waited until finally locks were unbolted, one after the other. The unbolting sounded uncannily like the noise you can imagine locks making when unbolted by the butler at Dracula's castle. The door opened to reveal a woman wearing a profusion of hair rollers, wielding a baseball bat, and asking suspiciously:

"What do you want?"

If it had been night-time we would have turned

and run. Since it was mid-afternoon, however, we felt compelled to explain ourselves:

"Erm, we booked a room at the Hope and Anchor?"

The woman put her bat down.

"Oh, it's you. Don't mind the bat – had a bit of trouble from the local kids last night. I don't take any nonsense, you know."

As if this would make us feel right at home. We followed her in. I can only put this down to the fact that we had paid for our rooms up front and we still had some hope that the situation would redeem itself. After all, this place was called the Hope and Anchor, right? We were shown into two adjoining rooms that had, a lifetime ago, benefited from 1960s utility furniture. They had long velvet-style curtains, bare forty-watt light-bulbs, and glass on the floor from the smashed windows. I am not kidding.

"I've made the beds up. You will be quite comfortable in here," our host explained.

There we were, two well-brought-up opera-singing girls and myself, wondering if we had walked into a rehearsal for *The Addams Family* by mistake. Having transformed to cheery landlady, the woman then asked:

"What would you like for breakfast – cereal or boiled eggs?"

Still stunned, we made our faltering choices, then she left us to a frantic conversation about how we were going to get out of the Hope and Anchor with our lives.

About ten minutes later, however, there was a knock at the door.

"Here are your eggs."

There, indeed, were two boiled eggs and two pieces of bread wrapped in cellophane, tomorrow's breakfast at midday!

"There's tea downstairs, if you like."

That was it. We made a run for it, smiling, saying that we had forgotten something in town. Once outside, we were running with our bags to the car. Tyres screeching, we never looked back. The girls spent their week's wages on a hotel room in a place that looked like a hotel and I ended up in a place called Newbiggin, so called because Old Biggin had been mined to the point that it no longer existed. The hotel was located right by the sea, with stunning sea views.

"Enjoy the view while you can," said my new, much friendlier host. "The cliff is crumbling and the room you are in will most likely be gone in five or six years' time." Not so much Newbiggin-by-the-Sea as Newbiggin-*in*-the-Sea!

It's so relaxing at the seaside.

No account of travelling woes would be complete without a few words about cars. Sue and I have found out a lot about cars by buying them. Here is something I learned: never buy a Vauxhall Chevette in the dark, in the rain, from a man who says, "I have never had any trouble with it. It's as sound as a bell!"

We took our dubious purchase home only to find in the cold light of day that a hole the size of my fist had appeared in the wing – a hole that the previous owner had thoughtfully filled with newspaper. You are thinking that no one could possibly be daft enough to do anything like that to a car. And I was daft enough to buy it in the dark!

I seem to specialize in bumping into people who are at the centre of really odd car-related events. I can't help it. I see someone in difficulty and I stop to help. Sue has got used to clambering into the driving seat as I rush out to lend a helping hand. There was the little old lady stuck near Putney Bridge in an equally antique Mini. She was very puzzled:

"I don't know what's wrong with it, dear. It stalls all the time. Been like that ever since I bought it."

I looked the car over, trying to work out the source of the problem. Ah, there it was. I spied her handbag hanging off a small lever marked in big letters: CHOKE.

"Why do you keep your handbag on the choke lever?" I asked, with the cause of her dilemma dawning like the morning sun.

"That's the handbag holder, dearie. I always pull it out and leave my handbag on it when I go out."

Problem solved. Although I am still unsure how she passed her driving test. Maybe the examiner was a fellow handbag devotee!

Another time, I was on the joy that is the M23 travelling down to Glyndebourne. I pulled over to help a woman plus her dazed mother, standing by their wreck of a car on the hard shoulder. I noticed that there were no tyres on either of the back wheels, just the metal rims that looked like they had been run into the ground. Feeling somewhat confused, I started my attempt to help with the old standard:

"Are you OK, love?"

Normally this phrase elicits all the information you need to get the ball rolling, and it did.

"I'm fine. I just don't know what happened. About fifteen miles ago Mum [who looked about 120 years old] and I heard this sound. We didn't know what it was, did we, Mum?"

I had no option but to put her out of her perplexed misery. Diplomatically I pointed out that the back wheels of her car had shed their tyres and she had been driving for some time on the rims.

I quietly dialled roadside assistance and had a gentle word with the horrified RAC man when he arrived. "Just be gentle with them," I said.

I think that we tend to look back with favour on cars that behaved well or on the ones that we associate with lots of happy memories, possibly blanking out the parts where we got left on a baking-hot or freezing-cold day on the side of a motorway with trucks whizzing past, inches from our feet. I hear friends reminisce fondly about the first car they ever had: "Oh, it was so eccentric, but it was my favourite."

Sue owned the first car we ever had. We did a huge

amount of miles in her old Mini 850, gigging with our band Crossword, usually trying to find the church or village hall where we were meant to be playing. Neither of us looks back with particularly misty eyes at that car. Four (mostly on the big side) adults, plus all our musical equipment in a Mini sounds like a joke already! We had to breathe by numbers: "OK, Sue, it's your turn now."

There were no windows at the back, just really high carbon dioxide levels. The Mini 850 had no power, no zip. The engine was open to the elements, so as soon as it started to rain the Mini would grind to a halt. We would dry it out and get another mile or so down the road before it ground to a halt again. We finally solved the problem with a judiciously placed sheet of kitchen foil!

Those were the days. In retrospect, we would probably have been better off with a carthorse. Both Sue and I have developed an unshakable predilection for cars that you turn on, and off they go. The Mini may be back in vogue but, surprisingly, not in our garage.

Over the years Sue and I have owned a huge number of cars and driven thousands and thousands of miles. We have accumulated countless dents, scratches and bumps on the cars we have owned. We would get a new car, say a lovely, reliable Fiesta, and one of us would be parking in an unknown, constricted car park and... bash! I travelled to Glasgow once and, fifteen minutes after leaving my car in a car park, I returned to find the steering-wheel on the front seat! We went through a spate of denting different parts of our cars but never the same bit. I went off to do a show, arriving back at my car to find someone had driven into the front of it. Sue went on an errand and bashed another bit. I finished a gig in Newcastle late at night and reversed into a pole I couldn't see. The following week I got a parking ticket driving to a show in London. I sometimes wondered if God was trying to get us to use the train!

Our favourite family car was a vast Toyota van, nicknamed The Veira Van by all the school kids. It had curtains and seats that turned into beds in case you wanted to live in it. It took at least seven passengers, bikes, dogs and musical instruments. The huge dental mirror dangling over the rear door stopped you bumping into anything you couldn't see and it would turn on a pound coin. We loved it and missed it terribly when we had to let it go.

I travel a lot, but I don't travel well. I don't mean that I collapse into fits of terror at the sight of a boat, I just get motion sickness. In spite of this quirk of nature, I still love fast cars. In my experience – let's say my experience of what Sue and I want in a car – I have noticed subtle differences between what I would call a *man* car and a *woman* car. Before you start laughing or throwing things, let me explain. Sue (woman), wants a car that is reliable and will make it from A to B without blowing up on the side of the road. She is not too fussed about the make of the car or how shiny it is. She does, however, want to be able to fit a couple of weeks' worth of groceries and lots of children's sports bags in the boot.

I (man) want a car that looks like a classic, perfectly preserved T Bird and goes as fast as you are allowed to go in the UK, with a speedometer that anticipates the sheer joy of really putting your foot down on an Autobahn one day in the near future. I want style, a car that says, "Look at me. How gorgeous am I?"

Sue would be happy if the car had a coffee-cup holder in which to stow her tall latte. I have, from time to time, tried to persuade Sue about the super-amazing benefits of owning a shiny sports car, to which she replies, quite sensibly:

"You can get one, if you can find one that has a boot big enough to fit in three boys, your electric piano, an amplifier, my mother and all the other paraphernalia you have to haul around with you."

At that point the only mode of transport that seems to fit the bill is the aforementioned massive Toyota.

Realizing my need for speed, Sue decided to book me on one of those "race a fabulous car around the track" days. I got rather overexcited travelling up to Stoke-on-Trent thinking about the throaty roar of a Lotus and the promise of abundant handbrake turns. We took out insurance, just in case I managed to break the Lotus, and Sue waved me off to the pits.

The first car I got my hands on was not a Lotus, but rather a long-suffering Peugeot 108, the racetrack's version of *Top Gear's* "reasonably priced car". Reasonably priced so that when the gears, brakes and handbrake are mashed, it doesn't cost the price of a thirteen-bedroom house to replace it.

I got into the car, passenger side, accompanied by Stoke-on-Trent's version of the Stig – a man who certainly knew how to wind it around a tight bend. After about a dozen handbrake turns, however, my motion sickness had motion sickness. After I got my turn at the steering-wheel and had thrown the car around like a rodeo pony, I felt like I had been riding a fairground waltzer for two hours after eating too much candyfloss. Hurlitzer all round. My Stoke-on-Trent Stig delivered me to the pick-up point for the Lotus and I promptly dashed around the back of a handy nearby shed to throw up, several times!

When I came up for air, cheery Stoke Stig roared up to me in the Lotus.

"Right, Jonathan, get in. We'll do the straights at 120 mph and this bend – here we go – we're taking this at around 80 mph, OK?"

I smiled, thumbs up and a little green. We pulled over again for a break before I got the chance to drive and I returned to the back of the shed. Then I got to do ten or twelve exhilarating, terrifying laps of the track, 90 mph into the bends, my head saying that no car was going to stay on the track at that speed. Sickness completely forgotten in those adrenaline-fuelled moments, I got a glimpse of what it must be like to race cars for a living. High octane. Then back to behind the shed!

At the end of my drive the instructor said, "You're a quiet one. Did you enjoy it?"

I have never been labelled "quiet" before!

Quite the strangest incident involving cars, plus Sue and I trying to help someone, occurred near Victoria Station, which is a stone's throw from *über*-wealthy Belgravia, Pimlico and Chelsea. It is also an area that attracts many people who are slightly the worse for wear.

On the evening in question, Sue and I were in the car on our way to pick up a friend at Victoria Station when we were forced to perform a driving-test-perfect emergency stop because there was a man lying in the middle of the road. The driver of the car that had hit the man in the road told us that he had been unable to stop as our blind-drunk, horizontal mystery man had lurched out in front of him.

When it was clear that we were going to help, the driver jumped into his car and drove away with his lights off, so we could not read his number plate. So there we were, left with a very drunk, semi-conscious man lying in the road, Sue trying to check if he had broken any bones.

Our hands were already quite full when round the corner, approaching the inebriated man, came a Humber Snipe – a big old car, weighing a tonne. I broke into a run, trying to flag the driver down and shouting at Sue to jump out of the way. The Humber Snipe, showing no interest in stopping, kept coming and promptly ran the man over again with Sue shouting, "Nooooo!"

The Snipe ran two red lights and sped off while we

went back to assess the damage.

Fearing that this must have killed him, we were amazed when the very much still alive drunk mumbled, "My wife will kill me when she finds out what has happened."

"I wouldn't worry too much about your wife," I said. "It seems like the whole of South London is trying to kill you tonight!"

Eventually an ambulance arrived and checked him over. It transpired that he was so drunk that his body was perfectly relaxed. He was able to get up and walk to the ambulance. Sue escorted him to hospital while I went to pick up our friend from Victoria.

"Some enchanted evening, you may find a stranger..."!

CHAPTER 9

Life as You Least Expect it

A good tale is none the worse for being twice told.

SEVENTEENTH-CENTURY SCOTTISH PROVERB

At the time of writing I have performed twenty roles at Glyndebourne. I am deeply grateful to them for giving me so many opportunities. One of the best opportunities I alluded to in the first chapter of this book. It was the fantastic role of Leporello, once again in *Don Giovanni* by Mozart. This was a famously controversial production by the opera producer Graham Vick. Not everyone had greeted it with open arms and a cheery word, but this was Leporello and this was Mozart at Glyndebourne, one of the famous houses for performing the great man's repertoire. I was doing one of my favourite roles!

Rehearsals had gone well and the whole team was pulling together nicely. The first night had come and gone and the reviews had been, on the whole, complimentary to the singers, if not the production. We entered night three with the customary sense of anti-climax. You build up to the first night. There is so much invested in this that second and third nights can feel a bit flat. This is not evident to the audience, but it may be how the performers feel. I walked on to the stage to perform the very famous "Catalogue aria" where on the command of his master the Don, Leporello shares some home truths with Donna Elvira. He informs her about the extent of the Don's infidelity (1,003 in Spain alone!) and that her cherished thoughts of marriage between them are basically not on the cards. The aria, which lasts six and a half minutes, is in two parts and is one of the most well-known in the bass baritone repertoire. The audience always anticipates this aria and rewards it, if sung and performed well, with great applause.

Modern opera theatres have many television screens dotted around the theatre facing the stage. To keep the spell of the drama, the TV screens enable us to keep an eye on the conductor without having to look down into the orchestra pit. On this night it was the lovely French conductor, Louis Longree, a meticulous and exacting maestro, but always a delight to work with. Once on the stage, I began the recitativo (the speaking bits, telling the story before the aria). I then began to sing my main aria, "Madamina". After about a minute, I looked across to one of the screens, stage right. Being hard of seeing, I squinted at the television as I could see nothing but a blank screen. I thought to myself, "Oh no, the camera has gone down."

But I continued to sing on into the aria, just listening to the orchestra alone, determined not to ruin things by looking straight at Louis. After four minutes or so, there is a new section and a tempo change, where I do need to glance at the conductor. I thought, "I will just have to look directly to pick up the new beat and look away again."

One glance told me what I really didn't want to know – there was no conductor in the pit! Louis had fallen forward into the violins and it seemed they had moved slightly to their left to allow him to fall while continuing to play. Musicians! You have to admire their capacity to concentrate. I continued singing for another minute or so until certain members of the orchestra and I became deeply concerned that he might have died. As I was singing, I was going over in my head what I was going to do next.

The French soprano, Véronique Gens, had no idea what was going on, as she was looking away from the front of the stage at the time, acting the part of the indignant young woman. In a very decisive way, and taking my life in my hands, I stepped forward. Stage management were horrified and thought I had finally lost it – the word "finally" being what worried me most! Advancing to the front of the stage, I started speaking to the audience. Please remember that at this point I was in seventeenth-century costume, singing to them in Italian, and much of the audience had not seen what had happened. They must have thought I had lost my mind, or that this was a stranger production than they had realized. I have to say that all my experience in public speaking had led me to this point. Speaking in my best Surrey accent (after all, this was Glyndebourne), I said words to this effect:

"Ladies and Gentlemen, I am sorry to tell you that, as some of you will have seen, the conductor has collapsed. However, there is no need for concern. We have the situation in hand, but I have to ask you, Ladies and Gentlemen, is there a doctor in the house?"

This was, of course, a phrase that I had wanted to use for the whole of my career! It being Glyndebourne, there were many wealthy people in the audience, but a shortage of people from the medical profession. One man stepped forward, however, and the curtain was swiftly brought down for an extended interval while this extreme situation was dealt with.

I went backstage and, loving a crisis as I do, sought to be in the middle of the storm, talking to as many people as possible and trying to brief them on what I had seen from the stage. Some ten minutes later, I knocked on Louis Longree's door to see how he was, or indeed, if he was still alive. I was admitted and he was lying flat out on his couch in the dressing room. I sat next to him, talking gently and quietly. He was clearly not quite with it, but asking questions about what had happened and the pattern of events, as he clearly had no memory of them. I explained calmly that he had begun the aria and that the next thing I saw was that he was lying face down in the pit. He asked me then how long I had gone on for.

Once again, quietly, I replied, "Approximately four and a half minutes, Louis."

At this information, he sprung upright from his couch, looked me right in the eye and said, now in a loud and confident voice, "Wizout me?!"

After half an hour's wait, Louis felt able to begin the aria again. So, up went the curtain, the audience applauded hugely and the show went on. I sang my aria all over again, this time with the conductor in full view, and to the clear appreciation of the audience.

The incident was recorded by many of the national newspapers the next day. I had finally made it onto the pages of the *Sun*. Success!

Turn to 2005, in a different context in a much smaller theatre – the Yvonne Arnaud Theatre in Guildford. My record company, Elevation Music, had organized a DVD recording of my one-man show, *An Audience with Jonathan Veira*. There were four cameras, a sound recording set-up and a sell-out audience for one night only. A lot was hanging on the evening.

I sat at home in the morning, some two miles from the venue, and my voice was just not working properly. I had about nine notes that felt usable and comfortable, and here I was, performing on my own for a recording! I was performing a huge variety of musical styles, from Donizetti and Gershwin to Billy Joel and country and western. I was concerned. Peter Martin of Elevation had invested a lot of faith and money in me, and it was up to me to come up with the goods so that we could make a saleable DVD. I spent the day working on my voice to increase its range and learning new songs to include ones that I could sing more easily on that day. This is when I first tried singing "Ol' Man River", and I have done it ever since.

Suddenly I was behind the stage and everything was ready to go. I had warmed up my audience, teaching them how to laugh and how to do a spontaneous standing ovation! I even had my ever-faithful make-up artist, Stella Olding, do what she could to make my face fit for the small screen. Sue had bought me a new jacket for the occasion and, more poignantly for this story, a new pair of shoes.

I waited in the wings, going through what had to happen over the next three or four hours. What to include? What to leave out? What happens if they don't laugh? What happens if the lights go out or the sound fails? My son Matthew was brilliant, running around, making sure everything was in place and that I was happy and relaxed. His temperament is one to die for in my industry. He is somebody you want around you at times like these, perfectly calm. Sue patted me on the bum and said, "Go for it boy!" I was up. I was energized. I was ready. The audience was excited and baying for my blood! The announcement came:

"Ladies and gentlemen, please welcome Mr Jonathan Vee-air-er." (Phil never could get my name right!)

I deliberately entered from where they least

expected me – the back of the stalls. Hurtling down the long flight of stairs, I came to cheers, laughter and applause. I ran up the steps onto the stage at super-speed and with typical JV energy. At which point – forgetting my new shoes with their smooth soles – I fell headfirst towards the piano. The audience gasped! I was on the floor looking like a beached whale and in that split second I thought:

"Brilliant! They're laughing at me already. Job done."

I got up, looked at them, and headed back up the stairs to the back of the stalls. This time I welcomed myself back to the stage.

"Ladies and gentlemen, Mr Jonathan Veira," I shouted into my microphone.

Cheers, laughter and disbelief. I ran back down the stairs, walked slowly and carefully onto the stage and put the microphone into its stand. This was all working fantastically, and quite by accident. I started to play the piano and suddenly the microphone popped out of the stand and clattered onto the stage! I gazed with incredulity first at the microphone and then at the audience, who were helpless with laughter. I picked up the microphone and ran back up the stairs to the back of the stalls!

Welcoming myself for the *third* time, I ran down the stairs, walked slowly onto the stage, put the microphone down safely and sat at the piano. Whereupon I was so out of breath that I couldn't sing for several minutes!

At this point Peter Martin, head of Elevation, turned to Sue, saying: "The cameras have been rolling for ten minutes. When is he planning to start singing?"

It turns out that this catastrophic beginning is by far the most popular moment in the whole DVD. As the Americans say, "Go figure."

The ability to improvise and make things up as you go along is a very handy skill to have if you are performing *Falstaff* in the open air or a delayed one-man show in the furthest reaches of Bangor, Northern Ireland. When you are performing anything, anywhere, some things are simply beyond your control – lights, microphones, music directors, fifty-mile-an-hour winds blowing through the tent where you are due to sing, the North Sea, cars, passport control, you name it. Let me give you an example.

When it comes to my own shows, I don't much like turning up and making use of a piano or guitar that has been provided by the venue, mainly because borrowed instruments tend to be really naff. This can present transport challenges when I have to get my electric piano, my guitar and myself from England to Bangor via Scotland and the Irish Sea. You are hardly allowed clothes on short-haul flights these days, so me turning up with a music shop is really out of the question. So, like the Vikings, who weren't known for travelling light either, I take the car and ferry.

This is all well and good if the Irish Sea is in a

happy mood. I had been booked to perform a show in the aforementioned Bangor. I have had a mistrust of the Irish Sea ever since I had my first real taste of it going over to Wexford in 1984. I was caught in the tail end of a hurricane and a journey that should have taken two and a half hours took nine! I was as sick as a man could be, leaving the contents of my stomach, and I am sure a few internal organs, bobbing between Wales and Ireland. Thus, I keep the ferry trips to a bare minimum. Sue and I drove the 440 miles to Scotland only to find that our ferry was cancelled. The staff assured us that the next ferry would be able to make the crossing, as it was a larger vessel and more stable. It is always reassuring to call the venue to tell them that the sea is not playing ball, only to have them confirm that they have booked a big hotel, paid a lot of money for it and people will fairly shortly be expecting *An Evening with Jonathan Veira*. That would be me, stuck in Scotland.

I get sick on boats, very sick, especially when the boat is pitching and rolling as badly as this one was, so it was a relief to get to dry land. Sue contacted Adrian, the concert organizer, whose faith had been stretched on a rack. Unbeknown to us, another ferry leaving at about the same time as ours had been turned back when a passenger had been taken ill. Adrian heard about this, but was unable to verify if we were on board this second fated ferry! Poor man – he was exhausted with the strain when Sue rang him. However, we were not "home and dry" yet. We now had a scant half an hour to make a forty-five-minute journey from the ferry to the venue. That would mean no set-up time. We had resigned ourselves to the fact that the audience would arrive before we did. I listened to *The Archers* on the way, hoping to achieve a Zen state of relaxation while I drove like the wind – illegally, I have to add.

Selwyn Hughes, the minister and writer, had a really good way of coping with travel stress. He said that when you find yourself in a situation that you cannot control, just relax. If you cannot affect what is currently happening to you, concentrate on making sure that you arrive well, not with your hair pulled out and steam coming out of your ears – especially when (like me) you have no hair to pull! This makes sense to me, especially because being tense while playing and singing is never a good idea. Many times, especially at churches or Christian festivals where the venue is being used for multiple events, you do not have the luxury of setting up and sound checking before the audience arrives. Of course, I always prefer to have a good sound check, but I have learned to roll with it and make the set-up part of the show if the circumstances take us that way.

"One, two! One, two!" then a jazz-funk version of "Once I caught a fish alive", other nursery rhymes and a couple of jokes to loosen everyone up, making sure the sound levels are right, and then off we go. I am so used to doing this now that when we got to Bangor, I started the show while walking through the audience with my gear, right then and there. I like to involve the audience in my shows anyway, so setting up with everyone there is more than OK with me. And sometimes, when you least expect it, something special can happen.

I love doing my one-man show. It gives me such flexibility and I love the contact with the audience. I sometimes pick someone from the audience to turn the pages for me when I am doing my stuff, playing and singing. I take some time to read the audience, work out who is sitting as stiff as a board, not moving at all, and who is likely to be happy to come up on stage and banter with me. There is no point in picking someone who is just going to wish the ground would open up when they come up front. I want someone who will be as happy as I am to play the fool. There is a film called *Mr Saturday Night*, starring Billy Crystal, about a stand-up comedian. The audience is laughing and having a great time, but he aims his whole act at the one guy who refuses to laugh. I can understand that, but it is not worth trying to get that guy onto the stage.

One night I was doing a show at East Cheam Baptist Church, reading the audience, waiting to pick someone to come up. After hundreds of shows, I generally know what to look for. There was a woman, I'll call her Charlotte, clearly enjoying the whole event, so I called her up. We had a great time up there, lots of fun all round. But afterwards, the guys who had organized the evening told me that the last person they would have expected to get up and work with me like that would have been Charlotte.

A couple of months later we got a letter from Charlotte. She had had a hugely difficult life and faced many challenges, but something special had happened that evening when she was called to the stage – the laughter, the banter, and the fun of it all, doing something completely different. I just picked her, Charlotte did the rest, but she said that night changed her life. God really does move in mysterious ways.

Imagine a lazy, sun-warmed, enchanted evening in the South of France, a moment when all the stars come out in the inky-black, velvet-cloaked sky, when the cicadas are singing along with the opera, and you are found to be sound asleep on the stage!

We were doing a production of *Falstaff* in a stunning medieval town up the twisty French mountain roads above Nice. We used the houses around the town square of Gattières as part of the set, the fountain as the centre point of the stage. I had turned up in an equally ancient big blue T-shirt that said GET IN GEAR in enormous letters, and the director was so taken with it that he had asked me to wear it as Falstaff in Act One. (Still got it – still wear it. Sad man that I am. Sue wants to burn it, but it is staying.) We were living in the gorgeous home of a local family. I fixed their piano over the six weeks we were there. *Très charmant.*

The local dignitaries in Gattières asked me to give a talk on the "Philosophy of Art in Opera" – a bit different to being asked to tell a joke while wearing nothing but a bath towel and some shaving foam. I managed this in my halting French with the help of my wonderful hosts, Mark and Françoise. It just does not qualify as a normal nine-to-five day, does it?

The production of *Falstaff* then moved on to another equally jaw-dropping setting, St Paul de Vence. The actor Roger Moore bought a house here after he fell in love with the town, and it was easy to see why. We staged our production against the walls of the old fortified town. Towards the end of the opera, Falstaff, having been soundly beaten, was to be found lying down towards the back of the stage while the fairies and then Nanetta, the Fairy Queen, sang. That equated to about six or seven minutes of me lying on my back looking at the stars. In France we started the opera at about 9 p.m., so it was now near midnight.

I was lying on my back, looking up at the stars, thinking, "This is the most extraordinary place. I can't believe I'm here. This is just so… zzzzzzzzz."

Fast asleep. The fairies were meant to prod me when they finished singing. I came round as a result of a series of ever more urgent prods and eventually a kick, as the fairies got louder in their entreaties: "Get up, Falstaff!"

More like, "Wake up, Jonathan!" I am meant to ask for mercy, and at that point, waking up with a start, I was not acting. Have mercy, please, fairies – stop kicking me! When the opera and all the thanking was over, the Mayor of the ancient French town asked for his special committee to come to the stage. In French he announced:

"Monsieur Veira, in recognition of the work you have put into making everybody feel so happy, for bringing something special to our town, we want to honour you with the Freedom of the Town. Please accept the Keys to St Paul de Vence."

I wasn't sure what he was saying at first but then someone explained it to me. The Mayor had gone to all the trouble of speaking to the conductor and the director and, as a result, I was being given the Keys to this amazing town. Among other things, I was now entitled to sit at the Town Hall. I went home that night to Sue, who had been with the children, so couldn't be there.

"Did it go well?" she said.

"I got the Keys to the town," I said excitedly.

"Very nice," Sue replied sleepily. "See you in the morning. Check the kids, will you?"

You cannot live on applause. It is good to go home and have the kids yell at you for taking their football away, or to go from a standing ovation to running the Dyson over the floor. I well remember finishing the first night of *Falstaff* in Copenhagen. I walked out of the stage door, having enjoyed enormous success and a cheering crowd. I'd signed programmes and accepted the plaudits of the management and individual members of the audience. I walked away from all the lights, the flowers and the laughter. Within fifty yards I was just a man walking down a road, buttoning his coat against the cold night air. While applause and rave reviews are wonderful when they come, the approval of God and my family mean the most to me. You cannot build or sustain a life on anything better than that.

To quote a line from a beautiful song called "All That Matters" written by Judy Mackenzie-Dunn that I recorded on my CD:

> *To find Him and His favour*
> *Is all that matters in the end.*

CHAPTER 10

The Final Curtain

Accidents will happen in the best-regulated families.

NINETEENTH-CENTURY PROVERB

I know many pianists. I know many *great* pianists. I have been privileged to record with many very fine pianists, but only a couple of them have become good friends – the really fabulous pianists Shelley Katz and Mark Edwards. One is a classical pianist and one is a jazz pianist – both are renowned in their fields and both are fabulous accompanists.

When Shelley sits and plays my piano at home, he makes it sing from Chopin to Beethoven to Bach. Even his scales are fabulous! I literally get a tingly feeling. Working with him on a couple of classical CDs was a total joy. Ken Blair was our producer and he and I would often sit back and luxuriate in the sound that Shelley would create. By day four of the album *Forgotten Memories* I had become quite ill and could not sing one of the songs in the prescribed key. Shelley said, "Give me five minutes," and we subsequently recorded the song as he transposed the music at sight. Awesome skill.

Mark Edwards is a man with whom I have recorded several gospel CDs. As a jazz player he has few equals in the UK. Mark achieves a level of harmonic and technical skill to die for. I will never forget when, at the end of a Christmas CD we were recording, I casually remarked that we should include "The Christmas Song" as a postscript to the album. He asked, "What key do you want?" I replied, "D flat major, please" – and in just ten minutes we had recorded the song that you now hear on the album. No rehearsals – no mistakes. Just a beautiful rendering of the popular song.

Both great pianists, both humble men. They are truly outstanding in their field.

When I play the piano I merely aspire to their level of greatness. Although I know that I could never achieve that level, it doesn't stop me playing. (Of course, it goes without saying, never in front of them!)

Even more weirdly, it doesn't stop me owning three pianos!

How many pianos does one man need? Of course, for those who love pianos, there is no answer – I guess, as many as one can have. I possess three at the moment and at one point I had four in the house. This from a man who, twenty-four years ago, had to borrow an old piano from friends who had no space for it themselves. It was a very old, seen-better-days piano, but it had nearly all the keys I desired to practise! It eventually found its place in our second bedroom in our London flat, but only after a

huge amount of reorganization and removal of walls
a very long-suffering and talented carpenter friend fro
church! After destroying much of the flat, he comforte
me with the lovely words: "It'll be all right, Jon, but don't
ask me to move it out again!"

On taking its position in our Streatham flat, I think
that piano drove the neighbours absolutely bonkers,
as the sound would travel up and, in particular, down
to the flat below. My good, long-suffering friend, Nick
Whitehouse, lived downstairs.

"If I'd heard you play 'The Entertainer' just one
more time..." he said to me recently. Sorry, Nick.

The acquisition of pianos is not always by intent but
sometimes through necessity and sometimes through acts
of generosity. My Bechstein upright was acquired through
necessity, and it was so wonderful to have a good piano
with all its keys and such a pedigree among pianos.

Ask any musician who has been playing for a
few years, and they will tell you that special musical
instruments have a way of finding their owners. One
day I got a call from a friend (In many ways more like
a sister), Judy Graydon. Sadly, Judy's mother (a piano
teacher for many years) had died a year previously and
the family had been scratching their heads over what to
do with her piano. None of them had the space to take
it, so she phoned me. The conversation went something
like this:

Jonathan: "Hi, Jude, how are you? How's things?"
Jude: "Fine. Just phoning to ask you if you a

interested in Mum's piano?"

Jonathan, not remembering what the piano was – thinking old upright with candelabra: "Jude, I'd love to, but we have two pianos already. We don't have the room. Sue would kill me if I even thought about saying yes."

Jude: "Well, OK. If that's what you feel."

The conversation then went on to other subjects until, approximately ten minutes later, with me about to say goodbye, I asked her in passing what the piano was.

"Oh," she said. "A Steinway, six foot two, rosewood, 1889, probably belonged to Lord De Rothschild. But if you are not interested…"

"You're joking!" I blurted out in disbelief. "How much do you want for it?" (In my head I was debating where I could put it. Three pianos and five people in a four-bedroom semi. Was I mad?)

"Nothing," she said. "I would just like you to look after it for the rest of your life and I would like occasional visiting rights."

Needless to say, I could resist no longer. I gave in and made my way to the kitchen to try and persuade Sue regarding the decision I had already made in my head. I was going to have a *Steinway* in *my* house! It was a dream come true and the beginning of Sue's nightmare of clearing a space for our newest acquisition!

The Steinway now sits in our bedroom while we sleep on bunk beds (just kidding!). I calculated that our, or should I say Sue's, study was thirteen foot by twelve. In one fell swoop I had gleefully managed to destroy her

office and find a home for our newest family member. Sorry, dear wife Sue.

Now to move the piano from Kent to Surrey. The BBC had just run a story about a prestigious, family-run piano-moving company that had been involved in an almighty accident while moving a seven-foot Bösendorfer from one concert venue to another. The Bösendorfer had rolled right off the back of the truck, the woman who owned it taking pictures as it slid majestically towards its doom. It was, after all, truly a Kodak moment!

"These are the people I want to move my piano, Sue!" I exclaimed.

"Yes, dear."

In my mind, the law of averages, or of staying in business, stated that they were unlikely to drop another grand piano any time soon. In particular, not mine! When the men arrived to install our Steinway, I told them that I had hired them specifically because...

"... we dropped the Bösendorfer and we were unlikely to drop another one?" said a man from underneath the grand. Over a cup of tea, I asked him what he would advise in a situation when a stately old piano like that makes a run for it. The polite version goes something like:

"Get out of the way, mate! What are you going to do to stop it?"

I could see his point. Half a ton of runaway piano is not something to be messed with.

Sue and I cried on the day the piano moved in – she

over the imminent loss of her study, me with the joy of welcoming a new member of the family; real tears all the same.

A Steinway has a life of its own. It breathes, the wood expanding and contracting with the temperature of the house. Sometimes one of the kids will come in and play, just have fun with it. If I look as good as our Steinway does in 120 years or so, I will be a happy man! The fact is, you don't really own a Steinway; you caretake it until you are gone and then someone else takes over the job. Now I can't imagine our family without it.

So I have told you about my two pianos – why the third? *An Audience with Jonathan Veira* is a kind of variety show where I do everything that I can to entertain people for two and a half hours. It started many years ago as a favour to our friends Howard and Sheila in their house in Guildford. They were inviting their neighbours in for a meal and wanted to know if I could provide some music and chat for thirty minutes or so. It has grown into what it is today, a one-man show that has spawned a DVD and hundreds of engagements throughout the British Isles. Essentially the show is based around the piano, though I do so much more now, including guitar and stand-up comedy. A piano of quality and preferably in tune lies at the heart of it.

Some thirteen years ago this started to be a real problem. I would arrive at venues to find pianos of, let me be generous here, variable quality. I would ask for a grand piano by preference so that I could see the audience. I turned up to one engagement where there was a rather old, beaten-up, upright piano sitting right at the front of the church facing a wall, with a big sign sellotaped to the front saying: "Do not move under any circumstances. The PCC."

I spent the whole concert with my head turned towards the audience at a ninety-degree angle, and a big osteopath bill to follow. Impossible! Even more impossible was the gig that made me decide (as Sue had repeatedly suggested) that we should buy a portable electric piano. I arrived to a lovely reception, a nice hot cup of tea and a fantastic level of anticipation for the night ahead. They had got a big audience for me and I thought that all was going terribly well. I sat at the piano, opened the lid and looked down. There was no middle C! I looked frantically at the organizer of the event and said in a now terrified voice, "Sorry, but there is no middle C!"

To which she retorted innocently, "Why? Is that important?"

I spent the whole night trying to avoid that hole in the keyboard! In the end my mind was made up. On Monday morning I made my way into Andertons, my much-loved and much-visited local music shop. I knew which piano I wanted, the Roland FP9, then selling (in 1998) for £1,600+. Lots of money, but lots of piano for your money.

"I want to buy a piano," I announced, "and I am not leaving until I do!"

With that I sat down at one of their finest and started

to play. Occasionally a member of staff would sidle up and make me an offer. "Too high," I would proclaim as I played on. I played non-stop until lunchtime. A crowd gathered. As it grew dark I left the shop very happy with my Roland tucked under my arm, purchased for £960. "A deleted stock item" was how they put it. Thanks, guys.

So, with my shiny new electric piano, everything should go without a hitch from now on! I should be able to turn up to do my one-man show without a problem.

Ah, but there is still the potential problem that arrives with the initials "PA" – Public Address or sound system. Or often, more like "No system at all – let's just hope we find someone to work it on the night." The whole PA thing sends shivers up my spine.

Opera is sung without a microphone. This, among other things, marks us out from pop singers. We learn, over a number of years, how to project the voice. That's the business. Obviously, when doing the one-man show or singing in front of 5,000 with a backing track, I have to use microphones. The backing track can make your life hell in many ways. It can refuse to play. It can jump about because it has developed a fatal scratch between the time you lovingly handed over your backing track CD and the time it is played. It can play entirely the wrong song.

Even if you carefully label your backing track CD with colour-coded arrows on a big label saying "PLAY TRACK 2" and your wife is standing right next to the PA guy, coaching him on when and how to play your track, things that can go wrong will go wrong. I was at Spring

Harvest one year with a backing track CD that had just two tracks on it, one with my voice, one without.

"Can you make really sure that you play Track 2, the Track that has 'NO VOICE' marked on it?" I asked very patiently, with years of PA-guy coaching practice under my belt.

"Sure, mate, no probs. You just walk out and I'll fire it up pronto."

Err, OK. Then I walked away from control of the final outcome, with no option but to believe for the best. My time on stage came, I walked out, the PA guy gave me the thumbs up and the track started. So far so good – instrumental opening. Then I started to sing accompanied by the unmistakable sound of my own recorded voice. Track 1.

I smiled as I was presented with the choice of lip synching like Madonna or developing a subtle harmony on the spot, so that people would not think that I sing to my own voice just in case I forget the words. The third, least desirable option, was to scream and shout at the PA guy in front of 5,000 people. I chose the second, harmony option. Grrrr. Smile away, Jonathan; think Christian thoughts. Jesus loves you, PA guy, but I will see you outside afterwards. Everyone thought it was great. Nobody learned from anyone's mistakes and the next time I sang, despite the even more explicit instructions that I had tattooed on the PA guy's right hand, it happened again.

You can prepare for a show as much as you want,

show up to all the rehearsals you like, fine tune your performance in every way known to man, make it to the venue in plenty of time, but you cannot always control what happens once you are on stage. I remember getting to one gig only to be handed the PA set in a box along with the words:

"Here's the PA you asked for. Do what you want with it. No one here knows how to operate it."

Four hundred people were booked to watch that show! Four hundred people who would not go home wondering why the people who organized the event did not know how to work their own PA system. In my mind this debacle was only going to end one way. It's a bit like DHL: no one is going to blame the van for breaking down, they are going to be mad at the driver. I'm the one on the stage, so guess where the buck stops?

Okay, so PA can be a potential problem, but that's it – right?

Actually, the real fun happens when the audience get involved. I like to keep my one-man show as flexible as possible and I am always ready to spend more time on something if I feel that the audience is really engaged with it. This can lead to some classic moments.

Little old ladies can be surprisingly lively. Don't let those sweet smiles and that soft white hair fool you into thinking they are pushovers. I was doing a show once, singing a range of my favourites including a song from Puccini's *La Bohème*. The aria is called "Vecchia Zimarra" or "Old Coat", a moving account of a young man's decision to sell the only coat he owns so that he can buy medicine for his ailing friend Mimì. I finished the aria, everyone applauded and the next moment a little old lady sitting in the front row piped up: "I didn't understand a word of that! Can't you sing it in English?"

Having a fondness for people who decide to get involved in my shows, I obliged and sang the whole thing again in English.

Still not satisfied, she then said: "That was all right, but how about something I know. What about 'Run Rabbit Run'?"

By this time the audience was helpless with laughter, so of course I obliged with a quick trip through the old wartime favourite. I went and sat next to her in the front row with my radio mike and together we entertained the audience for fifteen minutes or so. Lovely Flo, a woman in her late eighties, telling beautiful stories from her life. Someone wrote a poem about her, "In Honour of Flo", and it was with great sadness that I recently heard of her death. In the end, this was not an evening that ran away from me, it simply turned into something better than I had planned.

When I was younger – as you now know – music was my love. I also loved rugby and cricket. Still do. In my younger days, though, playing practical jokes was also high up on the JV agenda.

I would not blame Nick Jewitt if he never spoke to me again. Nick was a mature student, a painter and decorator who had decided to further his education by going to university. He had decided to study Sociology and I tormented him with the joke about his subject that was going around at the time:

"Written on the wall above the loo roll: 'Sociology degrees, please take one.'"

Poor Nick – he also had the great misfortune to be allocated the room next to mine in the halls of residence. Nick was broke. We all were, but Nick was particularly broke.

Because I am an inveterate practical joker, I decided to invent a prospective employer for Nick. Someone rich and very accommodating, the kind of person who would be able to offer him work at sky-high rates during our summer holidays. So, from the depths of my warped imagination emerged Mr McClintock. Nick would come back to his room to find scribbled messages to inform him that a Mr McClintock had called him while he was out. This continued for four days until one day, when I knew Nick would be in, I called him from a phone box (remember those?) down the road.

Me, adopting passable Scottish accent: "Hellooo, I want to speak to Nick Hewitt."

Obliging student: "Hang on, I'll just get him."

I waited, pumping money into the pay phone. Ten minutes elapsed. Finally Nick was found, and he made his way to the Common Room phone, located some considerable distance from his room.

"Hello, this is Nick."

"Oh Nick, this is Mr McClintock. I hear you need a wee bit of painting and decorating work for the holidays, is that correct?" (Still in Scottish accent.)

"Yes, absolutely, what do you need doing?" said Nick, rather excited.

"Well Nick, I've got six wee flats that need painting. How about I give you [I made up some ridiculously high sum] to finish the job?"

"That sounds great," said Nick, astonished. "Shall I come round and take a look?"

"No problem. I'm away for a few days, though. Why don't you give me a call next Monday? My number is 33446334."

"OK, I'll call you then," replied a bemused Nick.

"Oh and Nick, I hear you are a wee Christian. I was talking to your friend Jonathan Veira about you."

At this point, I was starting to hope that Nick would twig, rather than hang up thinking that he was about to be rich. No such luck. He missed the signals and hung up.

I got back to college to be greeted with the sight of Nick dancing up and down with glee.

"Jonathan! Some Scottish guy has just offered me a ridiculous sum of money to paint his flats during the summer. Can you believe it?"

Oh dear. The only thing for it was to let him down gently and prepare to run.

"That's great, Nick. By the way [turning Scottish accent back on], I hear you are a wee Christian?"

As the extent of my ruse dawned on him I made good my escape, although it took a fair amount of time and effort to elude the now furious Nick. I fully deserved all that I got.

Later, once he had forgiven me, Nick and I ended up sharing a flat. He learned that not only was I rather fond of practical jokes, but also given to an enduring state of untidiness. The pressure built and one day he tried to cure me of my bad habits by throwing every possession I owned, bar my record player, down the stairs. I don't blame him. Living with me is enough to drive anyone to desperate measures!

Having failed to learn my lesson, I continued to invent imaginary people and to make teasing phone calls to my long-suffering friends! One victim was my friend Roger Sutton, a Baptist minister.

Me, adopting passable accent of choice: "Hello, is that Roger Sutton?"

"Yes," he replied.

"Yes, hello, my name is the Reverend Farningham. I have your name from a number of very important people and I understand that you do a series of rather good talks on the topic of sex. How would you feel about coming to Surrey and doing, let's say ten talks for us? We would pay you, mmmm, £10,000 for the week?"

If you work for a church, you will know that this is an unlikely amount of money to be paid for doing anything.

"Jonathan," said Roger. "Is that you?"

Years later, by the time I was well established as an opera singer, Roger got his own back. He invited me to sing at a church he was visiting in Preston. This particular church seemed to attract lots of very kind, little old ladies. I duly sang "How Great Thou Art", Roger preached and then with a twinkle in his eye, he addressed the congregation.

"I hope you enjoyed Jonathan's singing. He is far too shy to tell you, but though he currently works at McDonalds, he is thinking of trying to make a career of it. Please will you take some time after the service to encourage him?"

I grimaced. He had me. I was defenceless. Several very kind, little old ladies later, I had to admit defeat:

"Okay, Roger, no more fake phone calls."

What goes around comes around. However, I chuckled when I realized that I was due to appear on *Songs of Praise* the next Sunday. I imagined some of those little old ladies:

"Edna! Look! Isn't that the man from McDonalds who wanted to be a singer? There he is, on *Songs of Praise*. It's a miracle!"

Never take your reviews too seriously. "A comic genius," said *The Times*. "A man with perfect comic timing," said the *Telegraph*.

Oh yes, I am the King of Comedy! At least, that is what I could have been tempted to think as the audience fell about laughing. But there is a saying about acting with children and animals.

I thought I was doing so well. It was the end of the first half of my *Audience with JV* show, but this time with my three boys playing with me. I was telling a joke before the last song and it was going down well. Really well. The audience was laughing fit to burst. I turned to my boys and they were rolling around, tears streaming down their faces, literally.

I finished the joke, sang the song that concluded the first half and went with the boys to get a drink in the interval.

"Look down at your trousers, Dad!"

Suffice to say, the trousers were fawn linen and I had been sweating so much that it really did look as if I had wet myself. Comic genius, indeed! Complete idiot, more like.

Kids. Who needs them? Can't live with them and you can't kill 'em!

All the trees in London seemed to be falling down during the year of the big London storm, while I was standing in a big, bright-green hospital gown emblazoned with the word "Father". Looking out of the window at Big Ben, there was storm enough in my heart, because Sue had been in labour for over thirty hours. It seemed that having this baby was God's way of preparing us for being parents: challenging, but worth every minute.

From time to time I hear people say, "We can't wait until the kids leave home." I don't get it.

Our kids, Matthew, Daniel and Nick, are the best things that ever happened to us. As I write, one has just got married, one is at university and one has just finished school. We still end up going on holiday together, even though I have an inkling that at their age they should be roughing it in a tent somewhere obscure. Maybe we should try roughing it in a tent and they will stop coming with us! I lost precious time with them when I was away on tour, but they have never complained, even though I'm sure it was tough for Sue and all of them some days.

When I was home I wanted to be a very present father and do with them as much as I could. I would drive them to school, collect them and drive them to various lessons and clubs. One day Matthew, aged six, sitting in the back like a bright little button, asked:

"Daddy, Mummy is very good at Maths, isn't she?"

"Yes darling, you're right, Mummy is good at Maths."

"And Pops [Grandad] is good at mending things."

"Indeed he is, Matthew."

"Nana is really good at cleaning things, isn't she?"

"Yes my son, that's why we have her round every Tuesday."

There was a brief silence.

"So Matthew, what do you think Daddy is good at?"

This was followed by the silence of a six-year-old boy thinking very hard, and then:

"No, can't think of a single thing, Dad."

Gee, thanks.

When Nick was about the same age and after we had finally given in to the kids' well-orchestrated campaign to get a dog, a cat strolled onto our front doorstep. You know, the way cats do; they have that artful "your house is my house" attitude. Nick was outraged and now he had the means to fight back: Bonnie, our new dog. Sliding a window open, Nick delivered this ultimatum to the mystified moggy:

"You'd better run, cat, run for your life. I have a dog here and I'm not afraid to use her!"

Kids have their own logic and their own version of how the world works. This was never more apparent than the day when Daniel sidled up to Sue to let her know his conclusions about becoming a parent:

"You know, Mummy, when I grow up I never want to be a daddy."

"Why is that, darling?"

"Well, I don't want to have to stand up and sing every day in front of so many people."

"Don't worry, Dan," Sue said soothingly. "Not every Daddy has to do that!"

"Really?" Dan was astonished.

It is entirely logical that our kids would think everyone's life revolved around music and the stage. If I was on TV, they would run around screaming, "Daddy, Daddy" for about thirty seconds and then go back to their Lego and a biscuit. When they were very young and later, in the school holidays, we would take them on tour.

I always remember the time that we took Matthew (aged three and a half) and Dan (four months) to Battignano in the Grosseto Province of Italy. I was there to take part in *Zaide* by Mozart and we had been invited to stay in an astonishingly beautiful Italian monastery.

The stage was set up in candlelit cloisters for the first night of the show, ready for us to start when it was properly dark at about 10 p.m. Dan was fast asleep in an old metal crib that our adorable host Adam had obtained from the neighbouring village. Sue and Matthew were watching the performance from an upstairs window, Matthew having convinced Sue that he was far too excited to sleep. As I appeared on stage for the first time, above the noise of the orchestra came the unmistakable voice of my young son yelling proudly in English:

"That's my Daddy!"

The Italian audience roared with laughter. Later in the show, my character has to attempt to climb a ladder.

"Daddy, don't climb that ladder!" warned my safety-conscious son, to more laughter.

My kids love the thrill of first nights. However, they have also had their fair experience of the shocks and spills that come with having a dad who dresses up and sings for a living. One spill happened when I was on my motorbike, on the way to play the nasty, abusive judge in a dress rehearsal of *Sweeney Todd*. This performance was to be the first in a sold-out run at Covent Garden and had a star-studded cast including Thomas Allen and the brilliant Felicity Palmer.

A woman stepped out right in front of my bike just as I got to the theatre, leaving her unscathed and me lying under my bike with a twisted ankle and a ripped tendon. As London walked by, I was forced to crawl to the stage door. Meanwhile Matthew, who loves musicals, had settled into his seat to watch the show – the sold out, now-delayed show – delayed because I was being strapped up backstage. A man walked out onto the stage to announce:

"Ladies and gentlemen, we are sorry to tell you that Mr Jonathan Veira has been involved in a bike accident..."

Matthew told me his heart just flipped. That is the kind of phrase you use when someone has died.

"... but, he has agreed to go on and craves your indulgence rather than your sympathy."

My judge was a pretty decrepit character, so it worked perfectly well for him to hobble about with a cane. Hobble about I did – it was even mentioned in the reviews. You would have thought that was enough drama for one show, but oh no! At one point, I was due to sit in Sweeney Todd's infamous chair and then disappear under the stage after my throat was cut. The chair was powered by hydraulics and was meant to descend from the stage in a measured way. I could hear the stage crew as they shouted to warn me from under the stage:

"Jonathan, don't come down, the hydraulics are not working!"

But throat slit and fake blood everywhere, however,

Sweeney pulled the lever and the chair descended, powered by gravity rather than hydraulics. *Bang!* I flew through the stage and thought, once again, that I had broken my back. The stage is a very dangerous place and I was beginning to understand why Daniel did not want to sing like his daddy.

Despite the spills, the music bug has done its job in our house and can be more than satisfied that it won over our kids in the end. There were sometimes tears during their piano practice, which I pretended to ignore but made me feel terrible! Now, however, I love it when they just play the piano or burst into spontaneous harmony as a joke. Our house has always been filled with endless opportunities for a song. On one occasion we were sitting at the lunch table, everything going nice and smoothly, until one of the kids spilled juice everywhere. There was a pause and silence when everyone looked at me to see what I would do. Suddenly, from nowhere, Nick (aged two) sang in his piping voice:

"There may be trouble ahead…"

You got that right, Nick – but we were all laughing too much to be cross!

Eventually, the boys started a band playing drums (Nick), guitar (Matt) and bass (Dan). Playing together was natural and easy – finding a name was the hardest part. After much discussion, Dan suggested that they call themselves Derek's Neighbour, in reference to our long-suffering next-door neighbour, Derek, who has put up with endless hours of band practice. We liked it – it worked – and Derek is thrilled.

When they can, the boys will join me on stage at one of my shows. Then we call ourselves JV and The Veira Boys. It's a bit like The Jackson 5 but without all the horror stories. They are all so different and bring a huge amount individually. As I have already mentioned, Matt is a great one to have on stage with you. A fabulous voice, and a great guitarist and front man – always ready to jump in for me, should that be necessary. Dan is our steady, dependable, rock-solid bass player – the middle boy and the central, steady fulcrum on whom we all depend. Every time I produce a new CD he sits alone and learns everything – ready to play! Nick is our "laugh out loud" boy – the wild and talented drummer who is a bit like a controlled version of Animal from *The Muppet Show*. You can rely on him to find the joke and carry it on behind me, so that when I think the audience are laughing at me... they are laughing at him. Love it. I have to be honest and say that when they play with me, it is one of the warmest experiences in my life as a musician. It is a moment when we can see from the response of the audience that they also love the dynamic of the whole family playing together, because we are clearly having fun. It's one of those moments as a parent when you think:

"So maybe I have done one thing right. Maybe a few tears over the piano were worth it!"

That being said, all my kids will rib me endlessly if something goes wrong or if the audience doesn't laugh at my jokes. We did one gig at Spring Harvest (normally a great audience for me) where I thought I had been transported to a monastery. I had no idea what I was doing wrong but the audience didn't laugh at any of my jokes – not even the funny ones. I gave it everything but no – they weren't having any of it. The interaction I had desired came later. In the car. On the way home. Sadly for me, in the form of Matthew, Dan and Nick laughing their heads off at me! "Dad, you tanked out there!" It's still a favourite family story that they love to tell, years later!

Why, oh why, would you want your kids to leave home?

If you think I can sing, you should see my DIY.

In 2012, IKEA plans to open its very first store in Croatia. All I can say is, *all the very best* to everyone in Croatia – you have my deepest sympathy. How, I wonder, did first-time buyers, students and middle-class people after a bargain ever manage to survive before the birth of IKEA? We go once every ten years to buy an extension plug, except you always end up with three because you never know when you might need another one, plus a generic picture, a pot plant and a rug that doesn't really belong anywhere but looks like a good deal at the time.

Oh, the psychology of IKEA! What doctor of the retail mind dreamed up those perfectly constructed rooms and the arrows (I believe IKEA management call it their Customer Guidance System – they are arrows, for goodness' sake!) that lead you like a sheepskin rug to the slaughter, all the way to the checkout? There a smiling attendant gives you the bill for your soothing retail experience.

"That will be £514.73, please."

What?! But we only came in for a packet of tea-lights and a set of plastic cups! IKEA is made for obedient people. For this very reason I like nothing better than to subvert the carefully laid-out floor plan by squeezing my ample body through a tiny space between Bathroom and Office, heading straight for the Swedish meatballs. Those Swedish meatballs are IKEA's secret draw card; you can even get them in Singapore, it's a fact. Swedish meatballs, an oddly tasty purple-coloured sauce, and mash, all for £2.49 in UK money.

The meatballs are IKEA's way of fortifying you for the time when you realize that the table and chairs, bookshelves and entire kitchen that you have just seen so beautifully constructed in room after room with soft lights and not an Allen key to be seen, will *not* magically appear, pre-made, in your home. Your new furniture will instead arrive flat, in cardboard boxes. You will manfully open the boxes, and pull out the idiot-proof instructions ("Should take less than two hours to construct") and more Allen keys than anyone should ever own.

You will battle plywood and metal for two and a half days. Then you will realize that you have three screws left over and your bookshelf will collapse. Then you will weep. You will be left wanting nothing more than to pack a suitcase and make your home in one of IKEA's beautifully constructed bedrooms. Or is that just me?

If you are completely inept when it comes to DIY, here's the plan. Move across the road from a kind plumber, electrician or painter, preferably all three, then make sure that you save your best DIY emergency for Christmas Eve, when you have fifteen-plus people arriving to share the festivities. That is what we did.

I can still hear my wife's scream from the shower: "Jonathaaaaan!"

Not good. I arrived at the emergency scene to find Sue hopping up and down in a towel while scalding-hot water sprayed out from our newly broken shower tap. Throwing caution to the wind, I did the only thing the man of the house could: I got naked, bar a pair of bright-blue slippers and some natty yellow Marigolds. In retrospect, it would have been simpler to turn the water off at the mains. But no, my brain did not stop at Logic Station – it never does.

I managed to wedge the shower tap back on while my naked body took a proper scalding; a temporary fix. We then did what we always do: we went straight over to our neighbour, Dave, who left his wife Tracey and his Christmas shopping to make sure our shower could not carry out any more of its devious plans for the boiling of our friends and family. What a blessing.

I have made it a policy to come back off tour to a DIY disaster. After I have kissed and hugged everyone and have given the kids their "Dad Has Been On Tour" gifts, the family will huddle around me, saying something like:

"We must just tell you this, Dad: for the last few days we've been hearing this *sussshhhh* noise coming from behind the oven..."

I would do some preliminary diagnostics that involve tapping things, only to find that the mains water supply had managed to escape a pipe and was now gently lapping around the back of the cooker. Then we would call Dave, who would fix the problem while asking very patiently, "Why didn't you just knock on my door when it happened?"

Bless him. Sue is now resigned to the fact that I make DIY disasters worse rather than better. She used to try to inspire me by saying Churchillian things like, "Darling, all you need is confidence. Just try it and you'll be fine."

Now all she says is, "Don't touch it, Jonathan! It will only cost us more if you touch it. Let's get Dave in."

One day Sue asked me to remove a small nail from an unsuspecting wall. Man up for the job, I got the claw hammer that her father had bought me. He had fondly handed it over to me, saying, "A man should never be without a claw hammer, Jonathan."

Sue's dad was a master of DIY. Not having any of his natural finesse, I yanked the nail as hard as I could and watched as six inches of wall came away with it. This gave Sue not very comforting flashbacks of the time in our first flat when her new, jobbing-musician husband, hoping to impress her, had tried to put a blind up in the bathroom. Sue's dad even bought me a drill for the job, handing it over with misty eyes: "A man should never be without a drill, Jonathan."

All that was left to do was to drill four holes for four screws, two on the left and two on the right. I had been thrown out (more like bodily ejected) from metal and woodwork classes at school. As I mentioned earlier, I failed GCSE Woodwork. Everything I made just snapped. No one fails Woodwork.

No worries. This was not GCSE Woodwork. All I had to do was drill four holes, right? Did I check the wall first, did I measure up? Did I heck. I glared at the wall, waved my drill in the air and threw the switch, whereupon the drill skidded along twelve inches of pristine plaster. No hole, just a very long, really deep groove. Hoping to save my new wife undue stress, I tore over to the nearest DIY store and bought lots of white Polyfilla.

"When you have applied your Polyfilla, just wait two hours before drilling," advised the cheery instructions on the back of the packet. Easy. Two hours and a nice smooth wall later, I positioned my drill for Round Two. The plaster had not set, however, so instead my drill now sent blobs of Polyfilla flying in a circular motion across the bathroom, landing like sticky snowflakes on the bath, the toilet, the walls, the floor. Blobs everywhere. The bathroom now resembled an installation at the Tate Modern. Should I clean it up or call an agent?

After several hours of hard effort, on top of a late night the previous evening, I was starting to feel really weary. In fact, I had reached that point of stress where the only thing to do is lie on the floor and hit it repeatedly with a hammer! So I fell asleep, then and there, legs sticking out of the bathroom. When Sue came home, she found me like that, drill in hand, plaster splattered everywhere, like a crime scene minus the blood. Initially she thought I was dead. When I came round she said only this:

"I'll get Dad in."

Sue's dad was such a lovely, brilliant man and he never made me feel like a fool. He just said encouragingly:

"You can sing, Jonathan – not everyone can do that. You get paid to sing – pay someone to do what you can't do."

Good advice, Sue's dad. We miss you.

And so we come to the erection of the Christmas tree. Many years ago, in 1993, a nice man from the magazine *Opera Now* asked if he could come and do an interview. He invited me to meet him in a coffee bar so that we could chat, but I asked him to come to my house in Guildford. The children were small, it was around Christmas time and I was performing in *Falstaff* for English Touring Opera. It had followed a kind of renaissance for me after the difficult period in 1989 with my illness. ETO had taken a real punt with me and enabled me to do one of my favourite roles, Falstaff himself. It was a fine production with Tim Hopkins directing and a great friend, Stephen Barlow, conducting (see the *Don Giovanni* with Kiri story). We had excellent press reviews, so *Opera Now* were keen on doing a feature on me.

Andy came round and we agreed to do the interview over a simple lunch. The children were typically engaging, making him laugh a lot, and Sue was her normal charming self. The interview wasn't really an interview. It turned into more of an afternoon and then an evening of just joining in with the Veiras. We talked little of career, voice, prospects, other singers or, in fact, what was going on in the opera world. It was a time when he became involved in the domestic life of the Veira family. Andy soon realized that I was not fundamentally interested in the machinations of my industry, but was someone who loved performing. However, he also discovered that I was useless at DIY.

The thing was, I had bought the Christmas tree to put up later that day, when he had gone. Given that he was still there at 7 p.m. and was probably going to be staying for dinner as well as lunch, as he was in no hurry to go, I said to him, "I hope you don't mind, but the Christmas tree needs to go up."

He carried on talking to Sue and playing with the boys while I struggled manfully into the lounge with the tree. As usual, they had not cut enough branches off at the bottom, and it was one of those new-fangled Christmas tree stands that require a degree in engineering and physics to secure it. I must have been huffing and puffing and getting close to turning the air a shade of blue after doing battle with this for nearly forty-five minutes. The tree now resembled the leaning tower of Pisa. As I cut more and more branches off to try and stabilize it, our traditional singing of "Oh Christmas tree, Oh Christmas tree, how lovely are your branches" seemed further and further away. It has been known, in the past, for me to end up getting a whole new tree because there were simply so few branches left that it resembled a twig in a bucket!

Andy walked into the room, shook his head and said, "Would you like a hand with that tree?"

Utterly shamed, but knowing that there was no way out, I said in my normal high-pitched voice, "Yes please!"

Sue, meanwhile, was in the kitchen, offering up a prayer of thanks and also rather grateful that the anticipated tree-lighting ceremony that the boys had been building up to for hours would happen.

Annoyingly, he took the hand-saw which I had used to butcher the tree, then took the whole thing outside and managed to secure it in less than five minutes. Yes, that's right – five minutes! Clever dick! Whatever, we decorated the tree, turned all the lights off in the room and sat around, as is our tradition, singing the words, "Oh Christmas tree, Oh Christmas tree, how lovely are your branches" – well, the ones that are left anyway!

The interview appeared some weeks later and he pretty much told the story. But what was so nice was that the portrait was of JV the family man, useless at DIY, but basically a nice guy who sings opera. I was happy with that and thrilled to have met him.

I was so pleased to have met Andy, just as I have

been delighted to meet thousands and thousands of people over the twenty-six years of doing this singing thing. I am not a party animal, but I do like meeting and talking with people.

As I try to find a way that is neither trite nor prosaic to finish this book, I am reminded of the comment that apparently I made (though it sounds too clever for me) at the end of that Christmas tree débâcle. Andy asked me what I thought about the profession.

I have been deeply privileged to be involved in the great calling to entertain people. It was inevitable for me, because I couldn't do anything else, and I hope I can keep doing it for many years to come.

The answer to his question, however, is based on what I believe has kept me alive and reasonably balanced. It is based on what is central and integral to my life – my faith in a God who exists and is involved and interested in our lives. He does not manipulate or control us like a master puppeteer, but gives us talents and abilities and says, "Now go and use them."

He also gives us people to walk the road with us – people like Sue and some close friends and family, who help to prove the point that what I do is *more than a job, but less than a life.*

CDs and DVDs

Jonathan's solo Gospel CDs

To hear all tracks go to **www.jonathanveira.com**

Travelling Songs (2011)

12 Gospel songs reflecting on life's journeys – well-known songs with the JV effect. Featuring "O Happy Day", "Swing Low" and "His Eye is on the Sparrow".

Elevation Music

You Raise Me Up (2010)

An inspirational mix of cherished hymns and popular modern classics, with musical arrangements that capture beauty and depth. Includes "How Great Thou Art", "Bridge Over Troubled Water" and "You Raise Me Up".

Elevation Music

O Holy Night (2009)

Jonathan teams up with the very best musicians to create an epic Christmas album. While retaining their much-loved charm, his beautiful renditions of timeless tunes provide a fresh way of celebrating the wonders of this season. Highlights include "O Holy Night", "Joy to the World" and "Thorns in the Straw".

Elevation Music

Pilgrim (2008)

This is a fabulous "crossover" album. Songs originally penned or sung by artists including Bob Dylan, Louis Armstrong, Coldplay, Van Morrison, Bryn Haworth and Chris Eaton, now performed by one of the finest voices in contemporary music.

Elevation Music

All That Matters (2006)

This fourth Gospel album from JV has received much acclaim. Jonathan has aimed to include a jazz/blues/Gospel feel displaying the funkier side of his character here.

Elevation Music

Rhythms of the Heart (2004)

Rhythms Of The Heart is a warm, contemplative album full of intimate and heartfelt performances. Jonathan mixes classic hymns such as "How Great Thou Art" and "The

Day Thou Gavest", with modern worship songs, many written by Paul Field.
Elevation Music

Life and Soul (2001)

This outstanding recording contains a variety of songs including the ever-popular "King of Kings, Majesty" as seen on the BBC's *Songs of Praise* 40th Anniversary Gala Evening.
Elevation Music

An Audience with Jonathan Veira DVD (2005)

If you want to enjoy JV at his very best, there is no better way than to "be there live" at one of his one-man shows. However, the next best thing is to get hold of the DVD *An Audience with Jonathan Veira*.
Elevation Music

BBC RECORDINGS

Songs of Praise – Your Favourite Hymns and Music (2001)

Jonathan sings the nation's favourite hymn "How Great Thou Art" during the BBC *Songs of Praise* 40th Anniversary.
BBC Music

Songs of Praise – Hymns from the Holy Land (2000)

Jonathan sings five hymns alongside various artists. Performed in Jerusalem in 2000 for the Easter *Songs of Praise* programme.
BBC Music

CLASSICAL RECORDINGS

Jeffreys: Idylls and Elegies (2010)

Jonathan performs three solo items.
Divine Art

A Century of English Song, Vol. 3 (2001)

Featuring songs by Ivor Gurney, Peter Warlock, Roger Quilter.
With Jonathan Veira (baritone), Sarah Leonard (soprano), and Malcolm Martineau (piano).
Somm Music

Jeffreys: Of Fire and Dew (2001)

21 English songs composed by John Jeffreys.
Jonathan Veira (baritone) sings with Shelley Katz (piano).

Somm Music

OPERA RECORDINGS

The Marriage of Figaro – Mozart (2004)

Jonathan as Dr Bartolo (baritone)

Chandos Music

La Vedova Scaltra – Wolf Ferrari (2004)

Jonathan as Don Alvaro.

Accord

Jenufa – Janacek

Covent Garden (2001)
Jonathan plays the part of Starek (Mill owner).

Erato

Rose of Persia – Arthur Sullivan (1999)

Jonathan plays the part of Abdallah.

Cpo for The BBC Music Magazine

OPERA DVDS

Le Nozze di Figaro – Mozart DVD (2006)

Royal Opera House
Jonathan as Dr Bartolo.

Opus Arte

Lulu – Berg DVD (1996)

Glyndebourne Festival Opera
Jonathan plays various roles.

Warner Classics